# ABSTRACT

# DESIGN

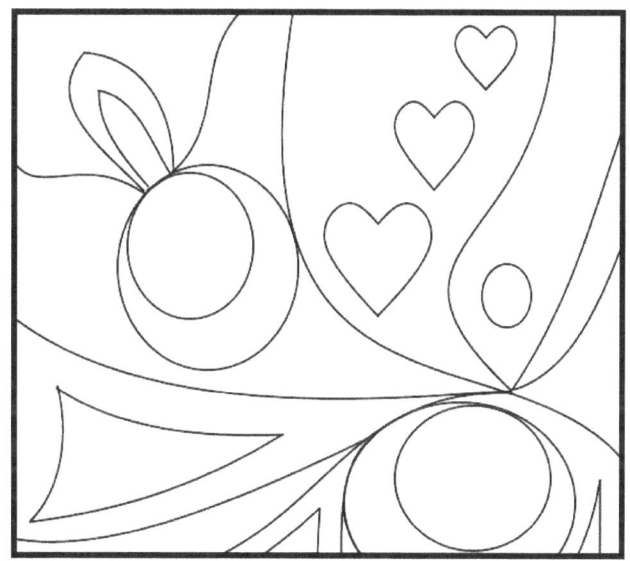

# Coloring Book

## Designed for Use with Bright Colors

### Original Hand Drawn Images for Relaxation

By: Kaye Dennan

KD Coloring Studio

http://kdcoloring.com

ISBN-13: 978-1541061583

**Paperback Edition**

Manufactured in the United States of America

# Sample Images from this Book

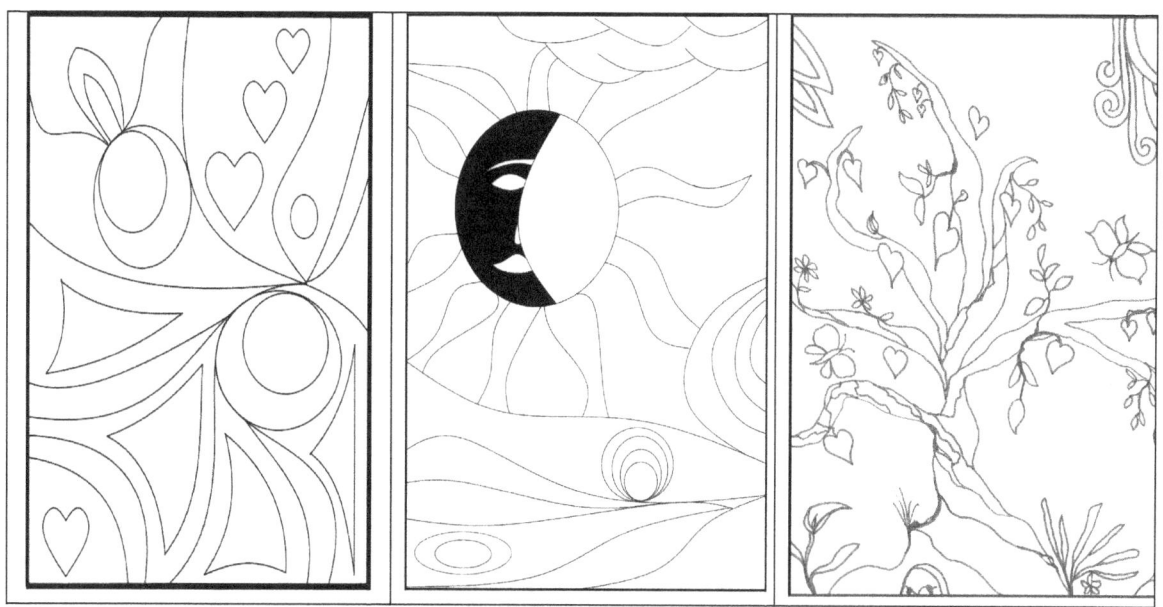

## PUBLISHERS NOTES
### Disclaimer

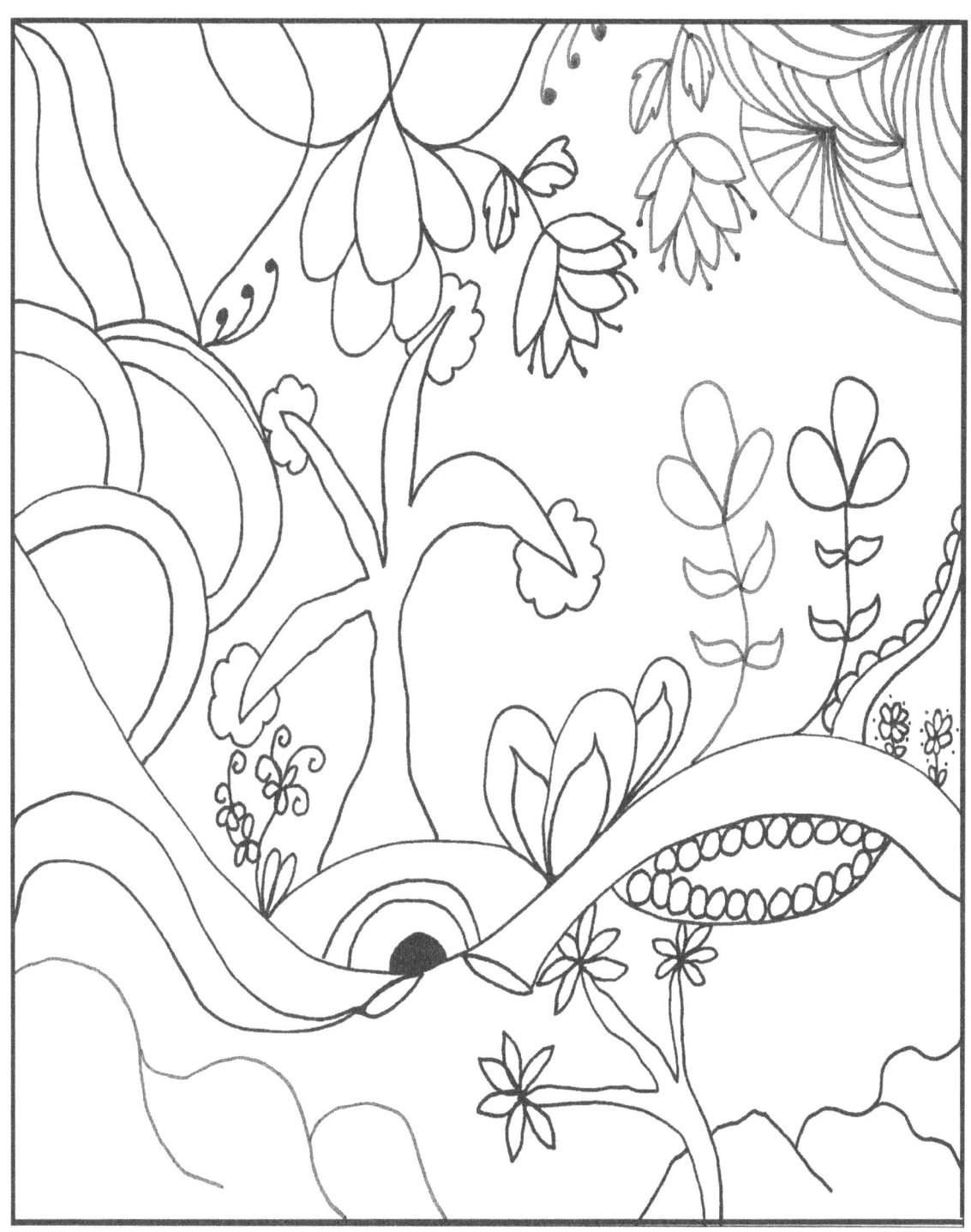

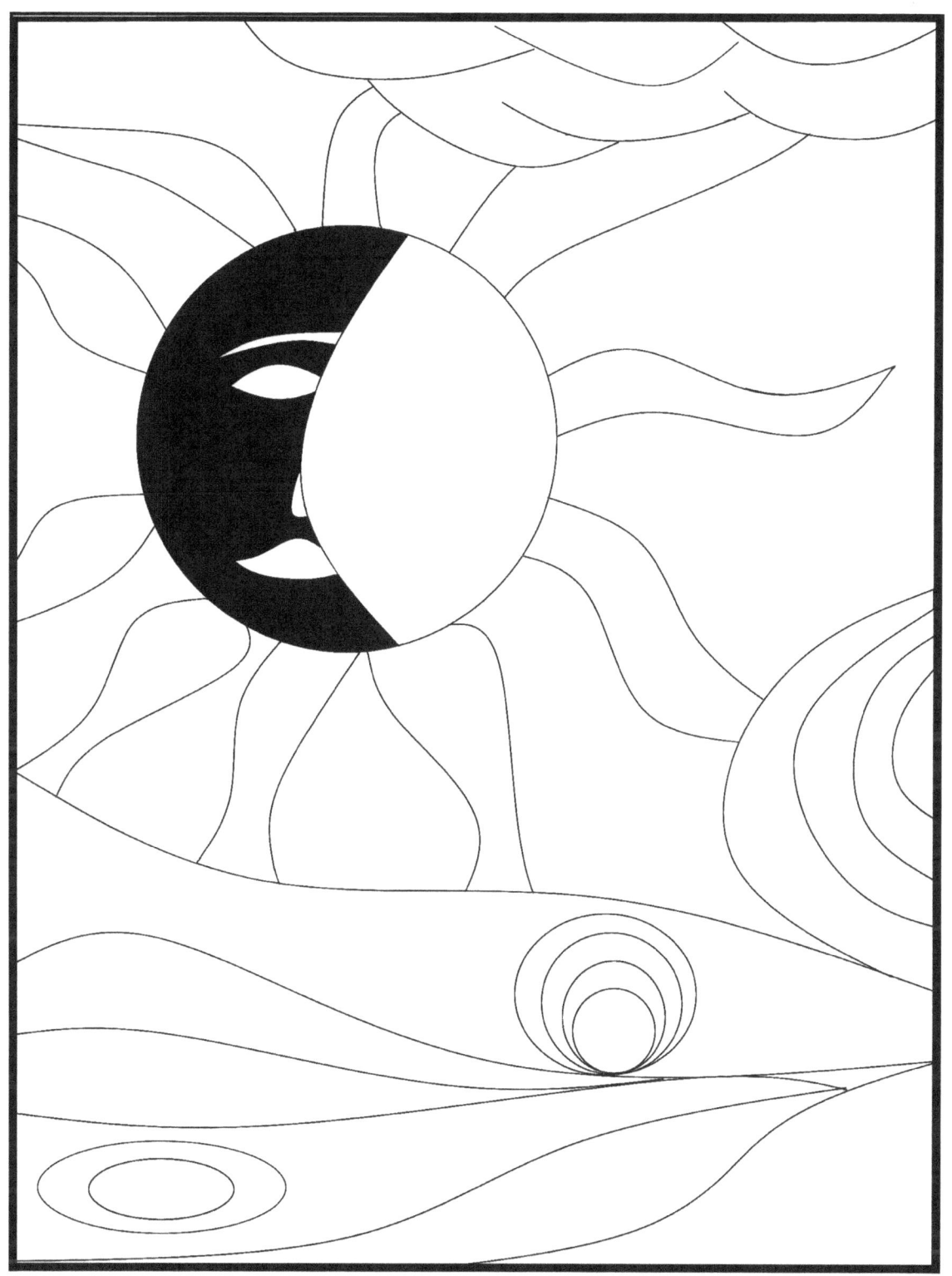

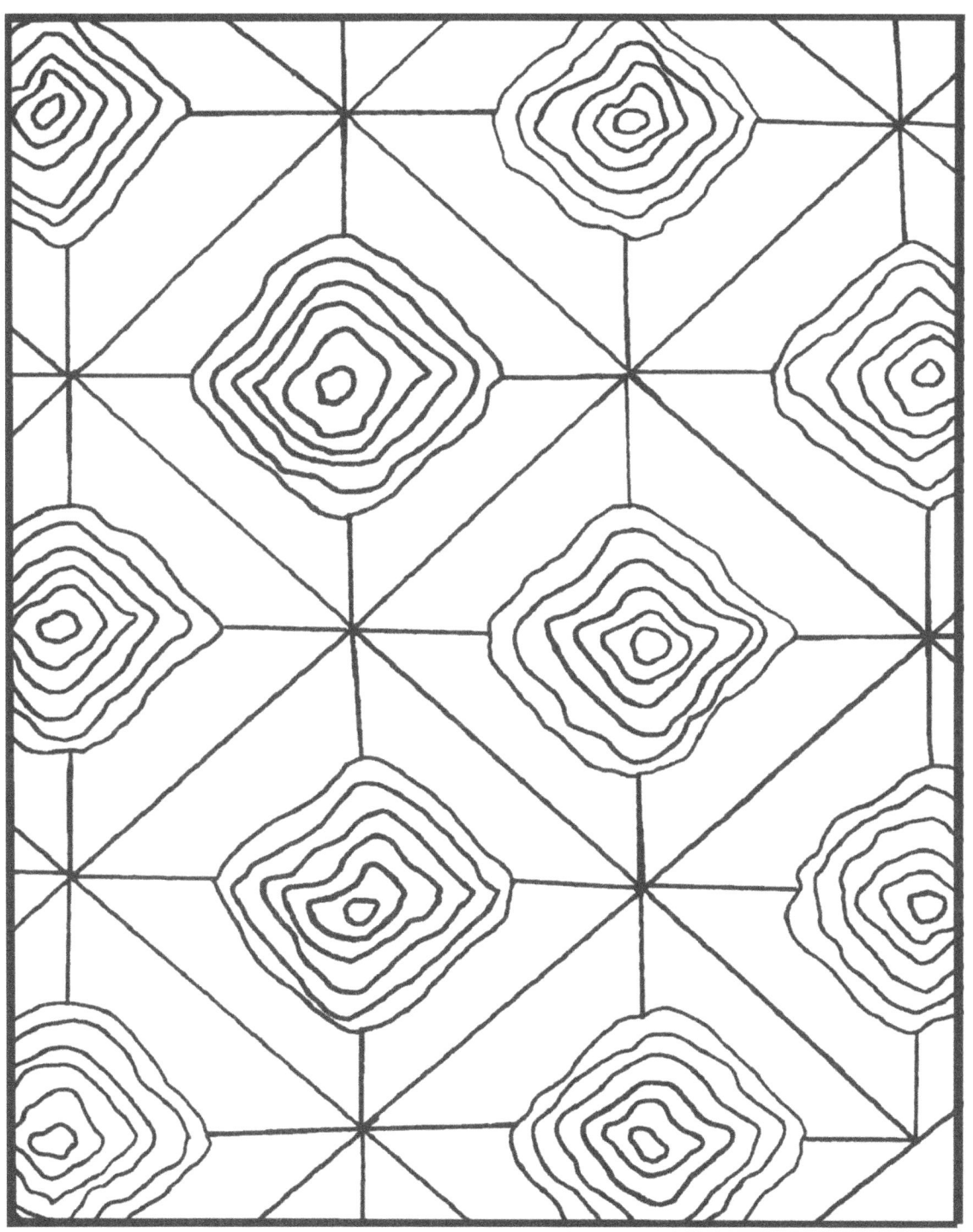

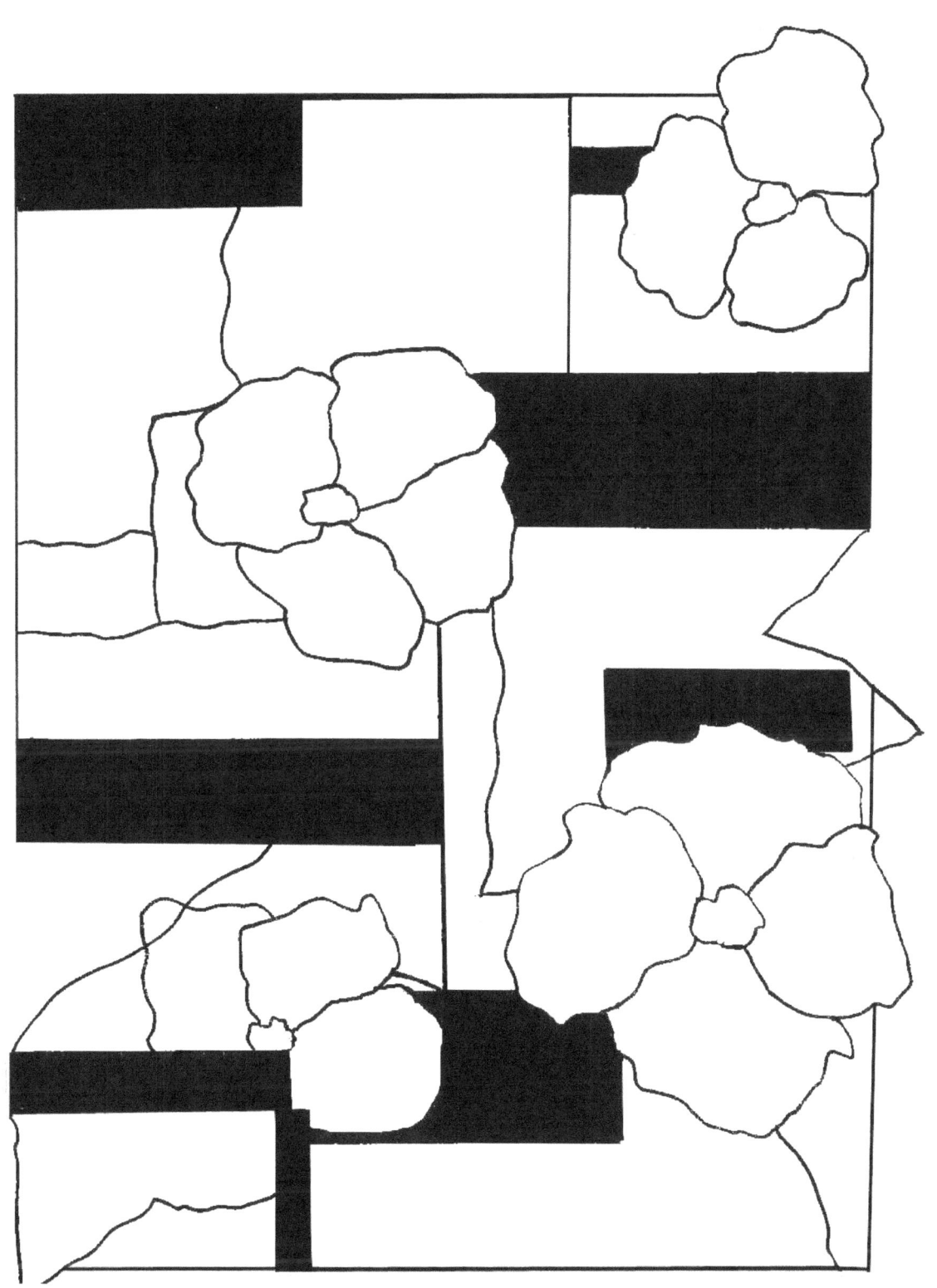

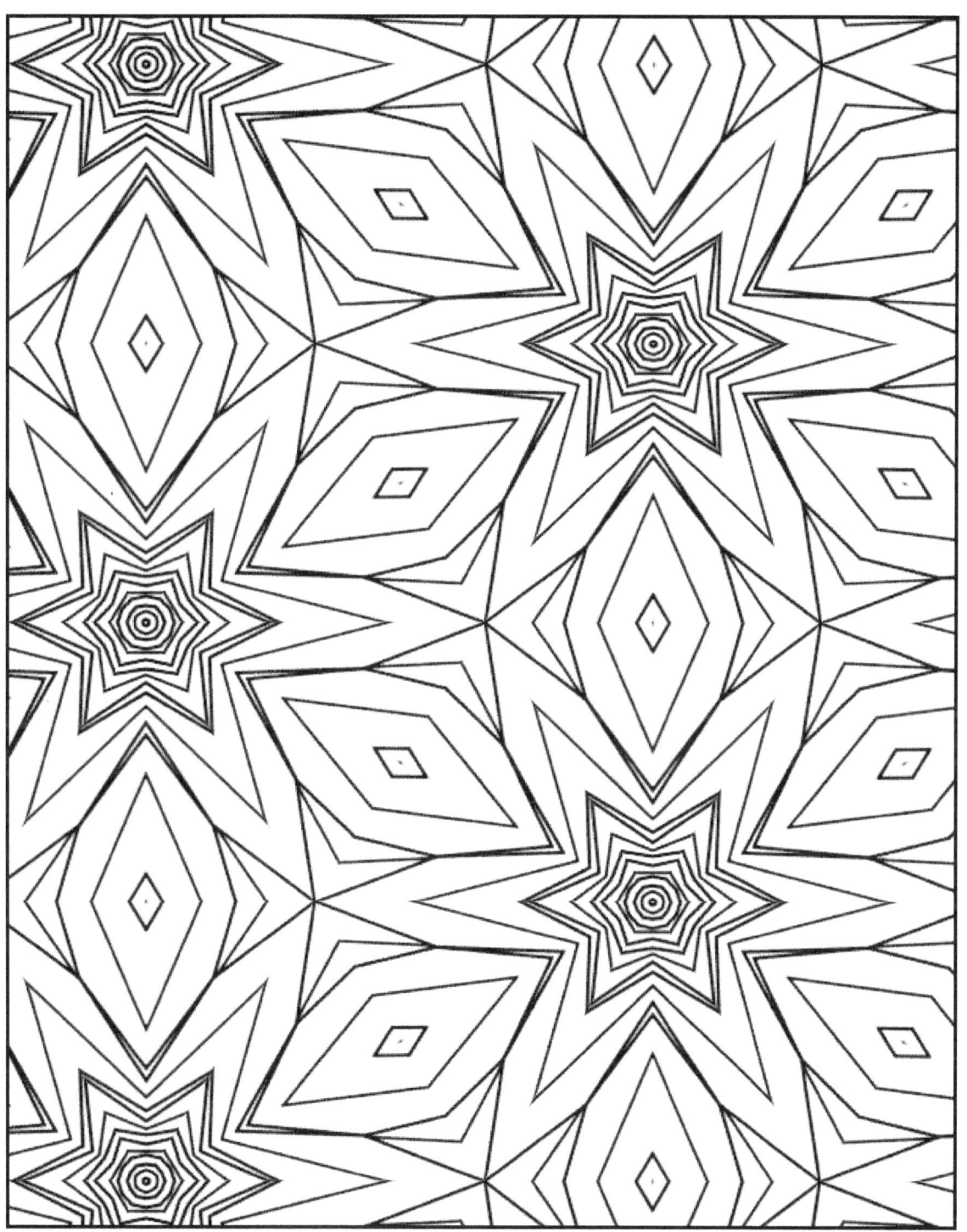

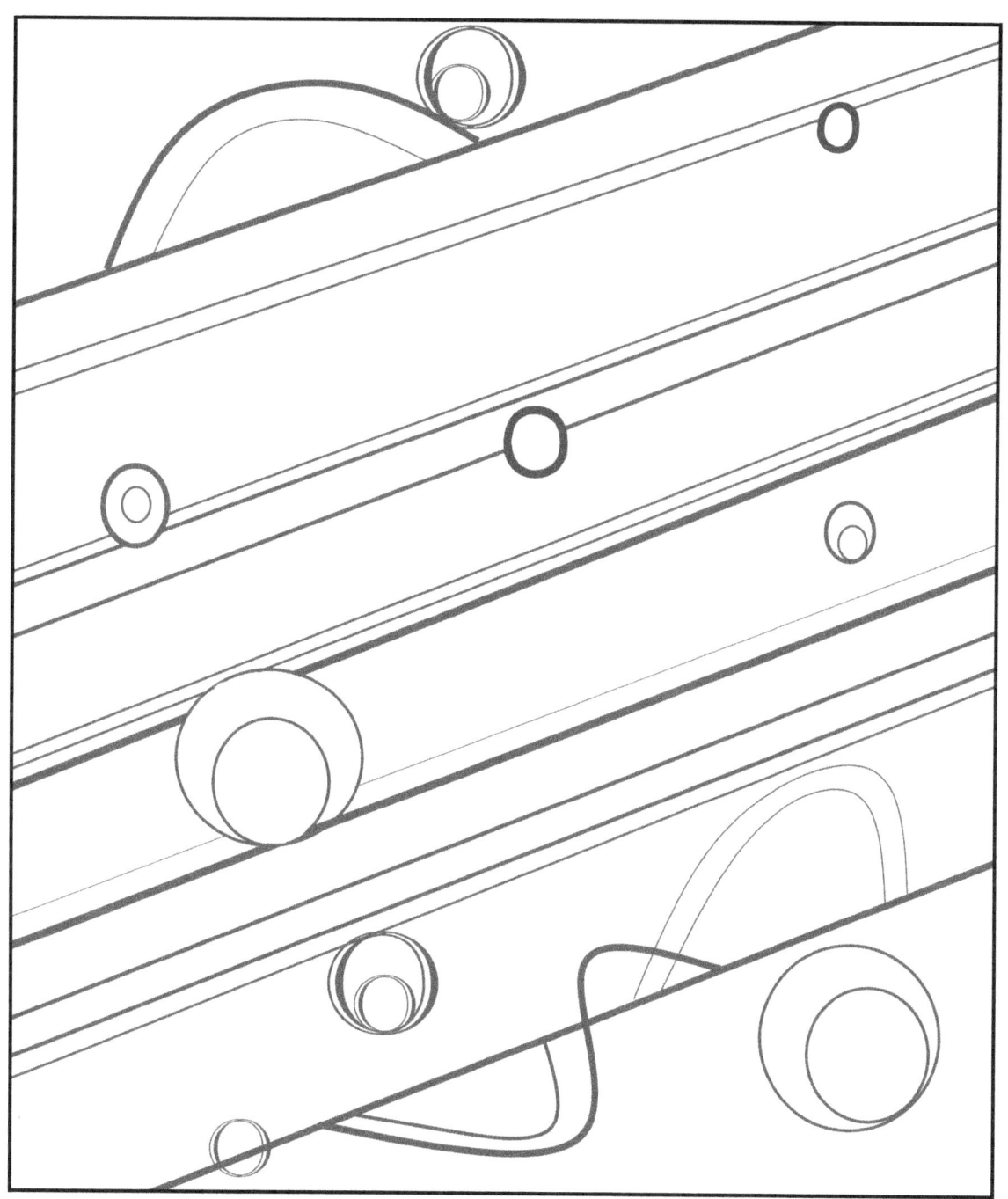

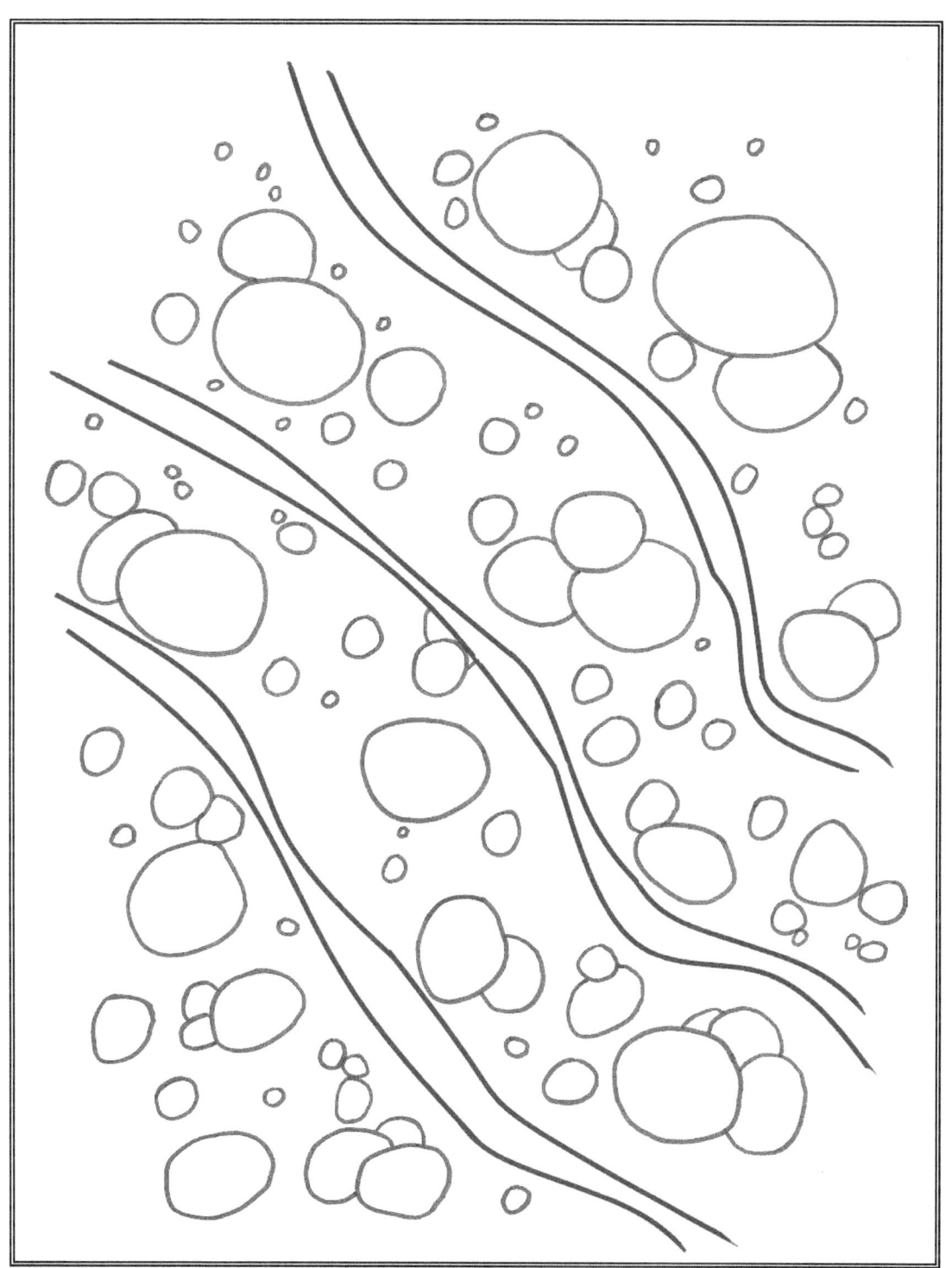

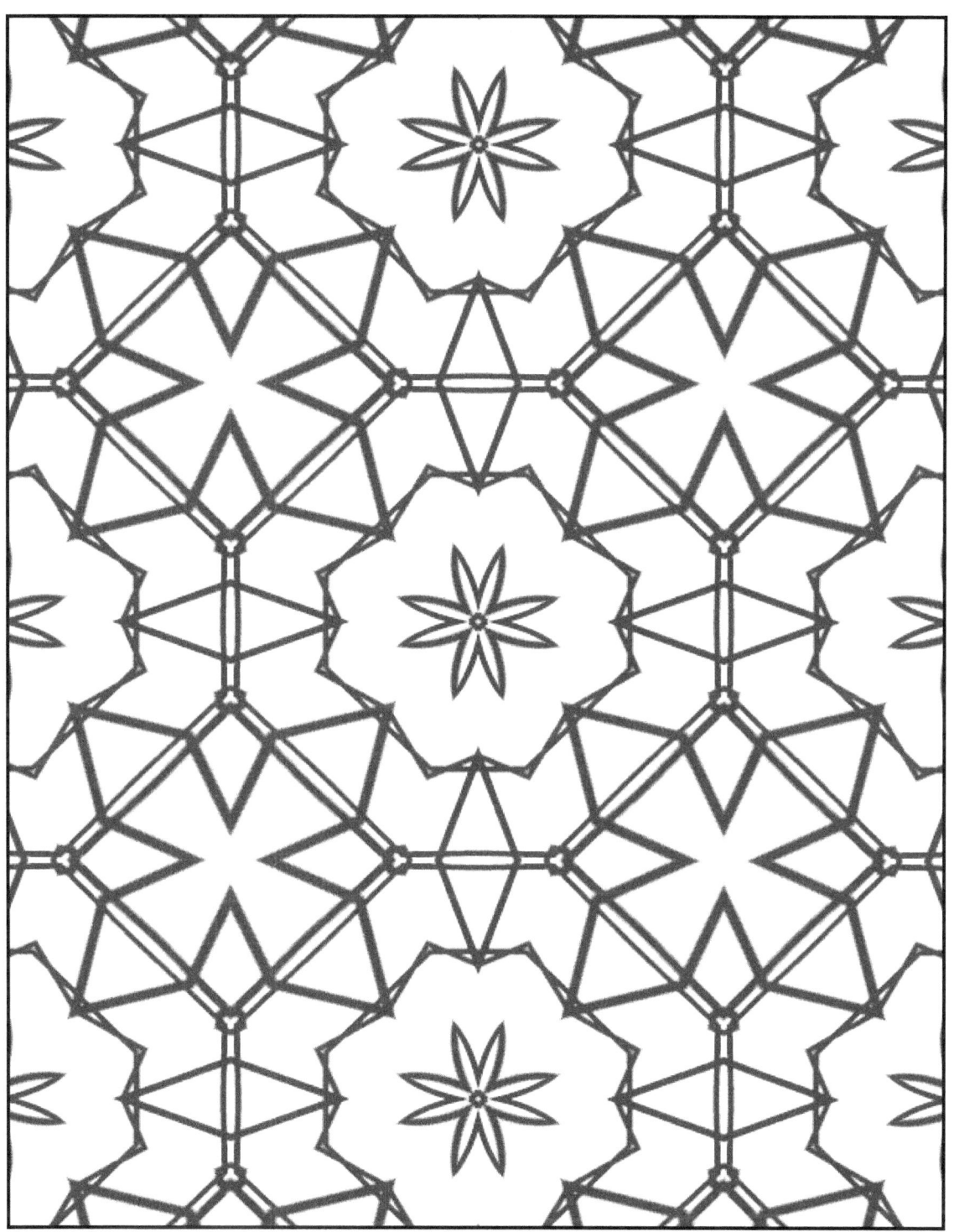

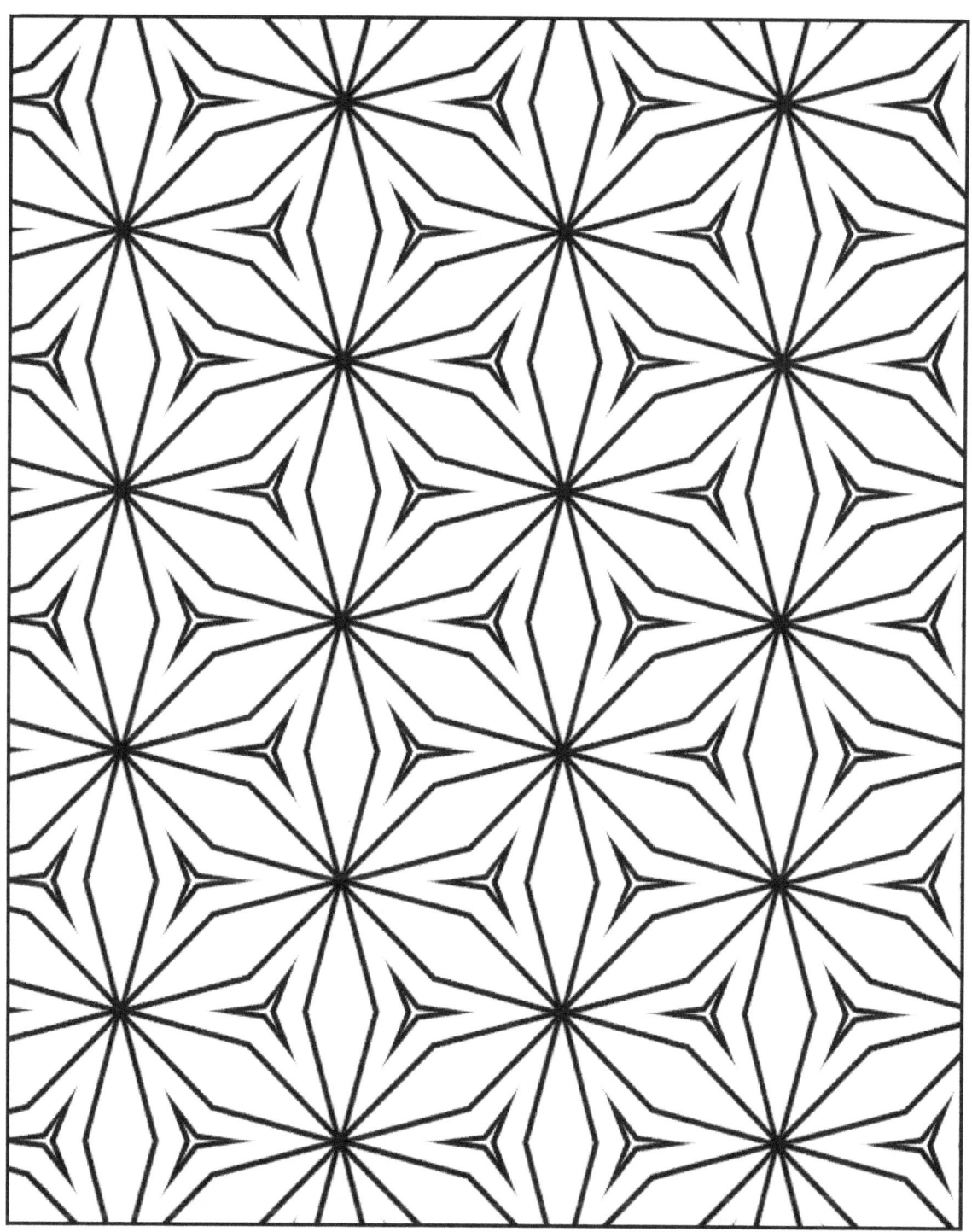

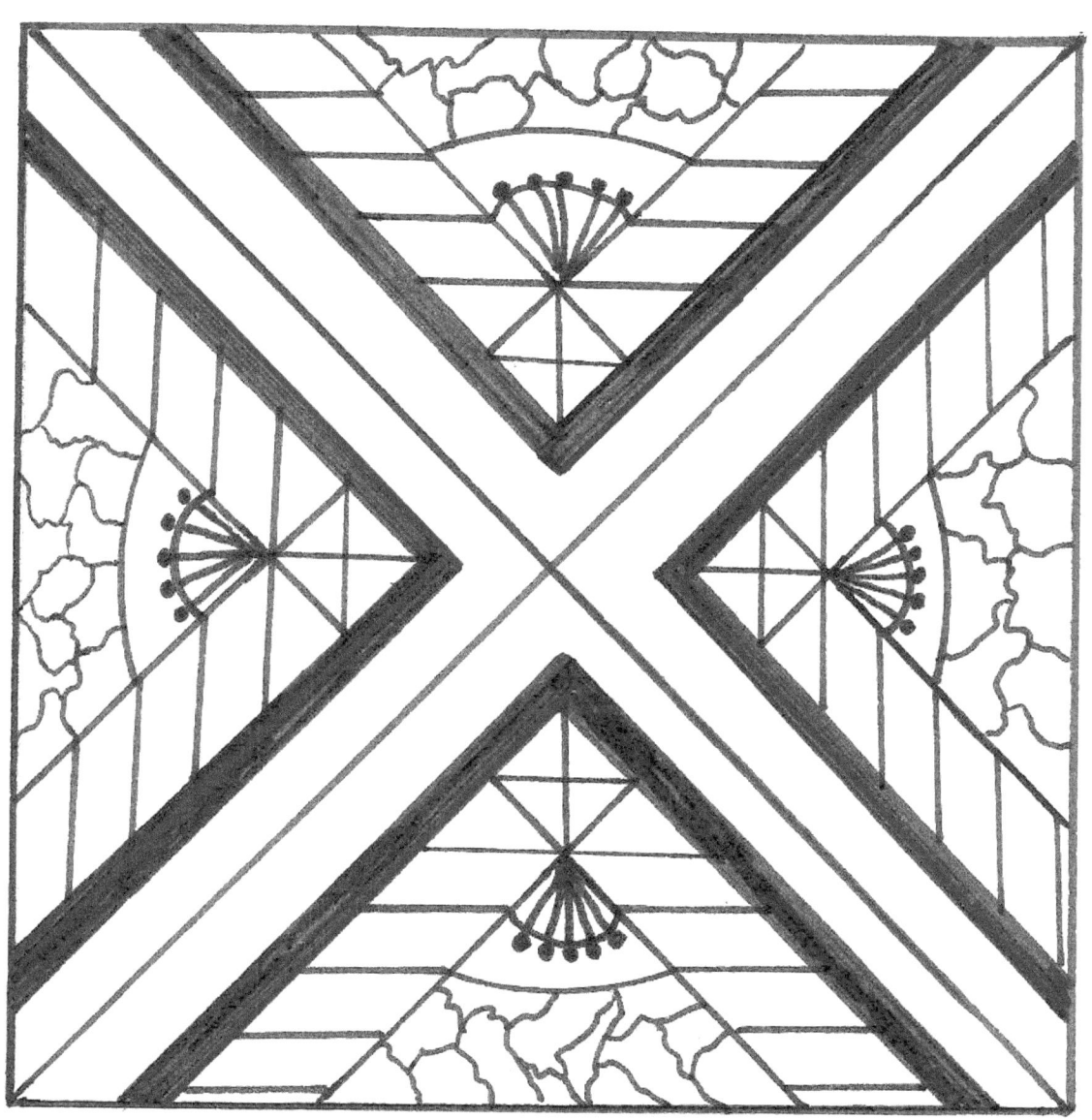

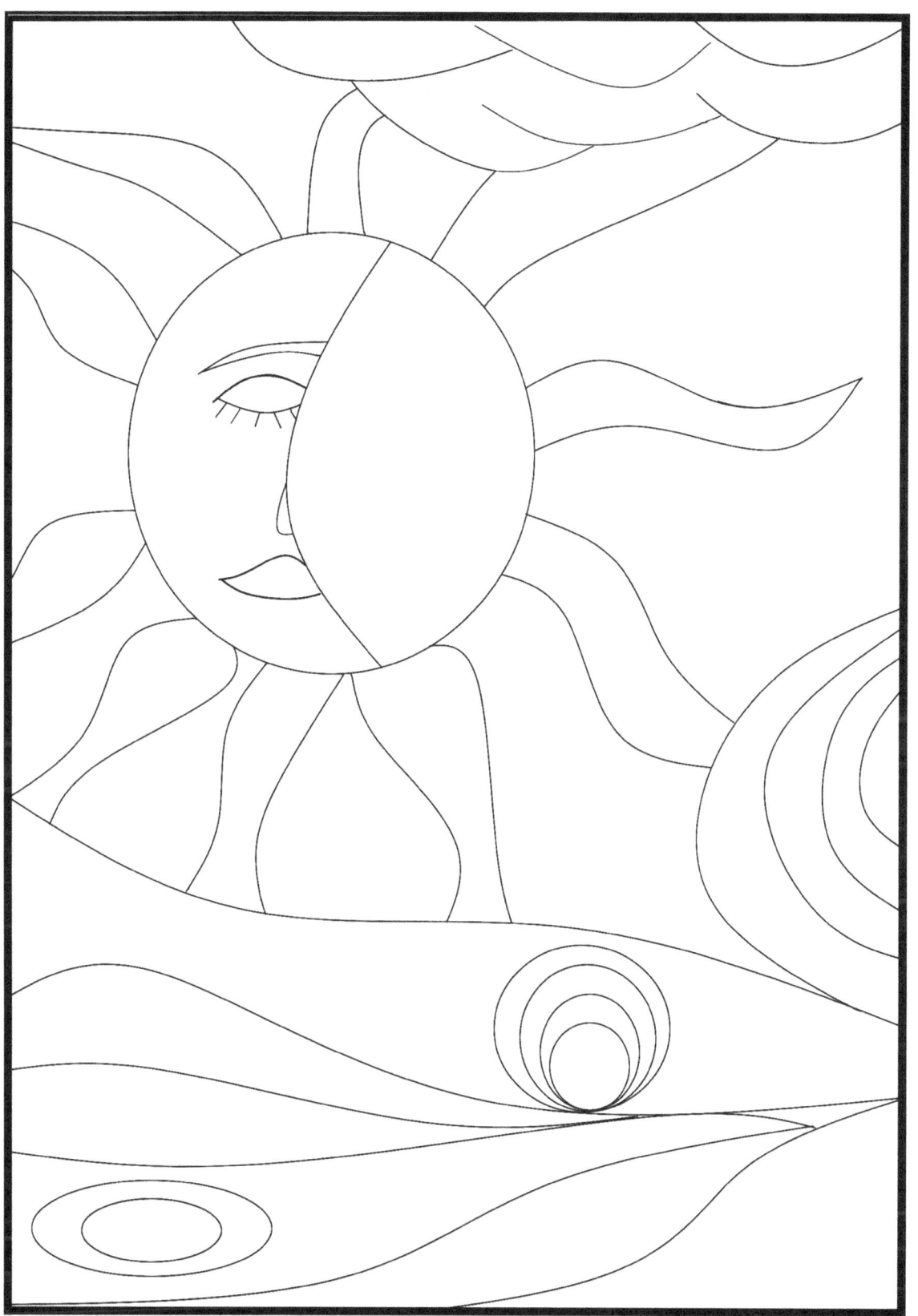

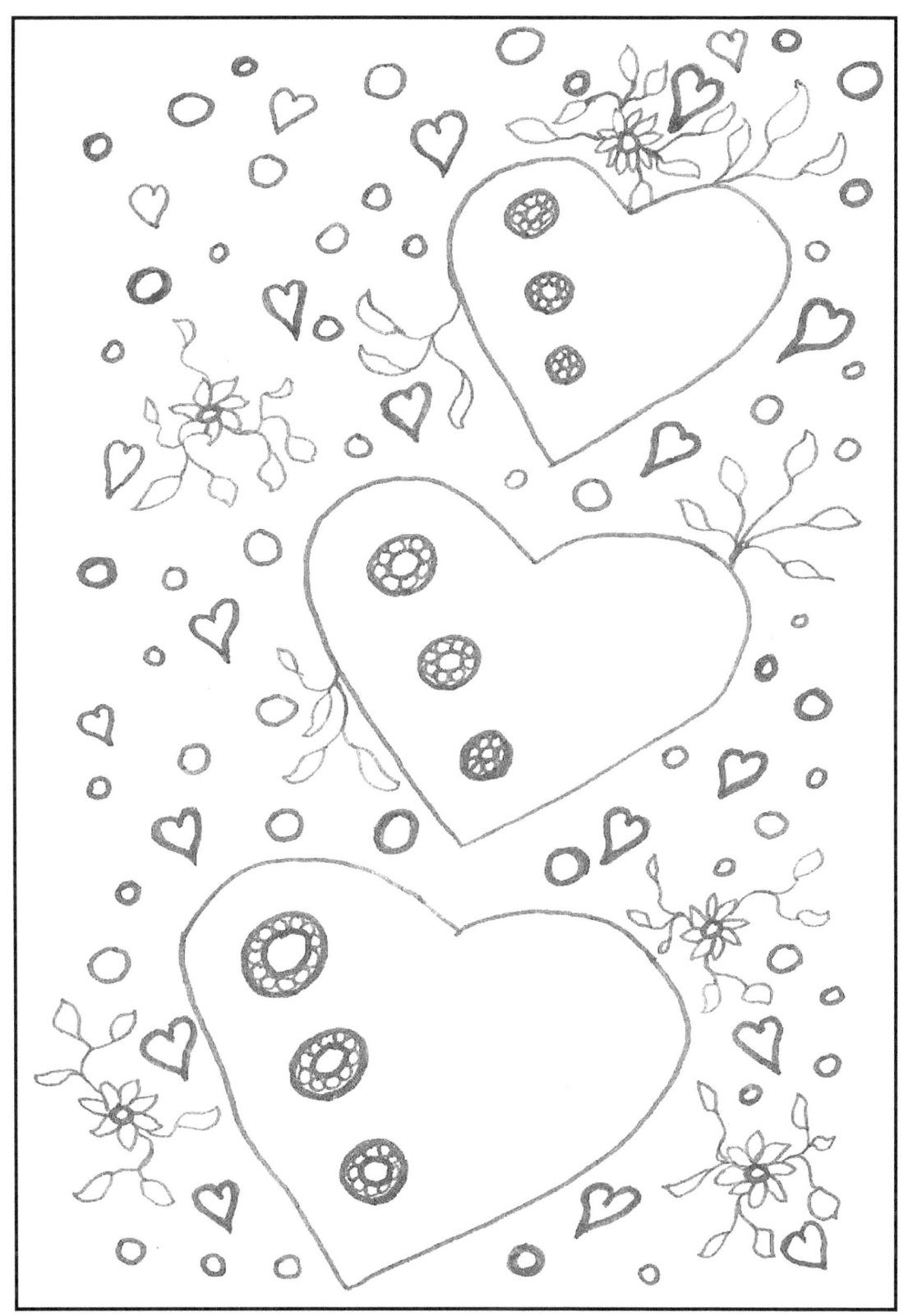

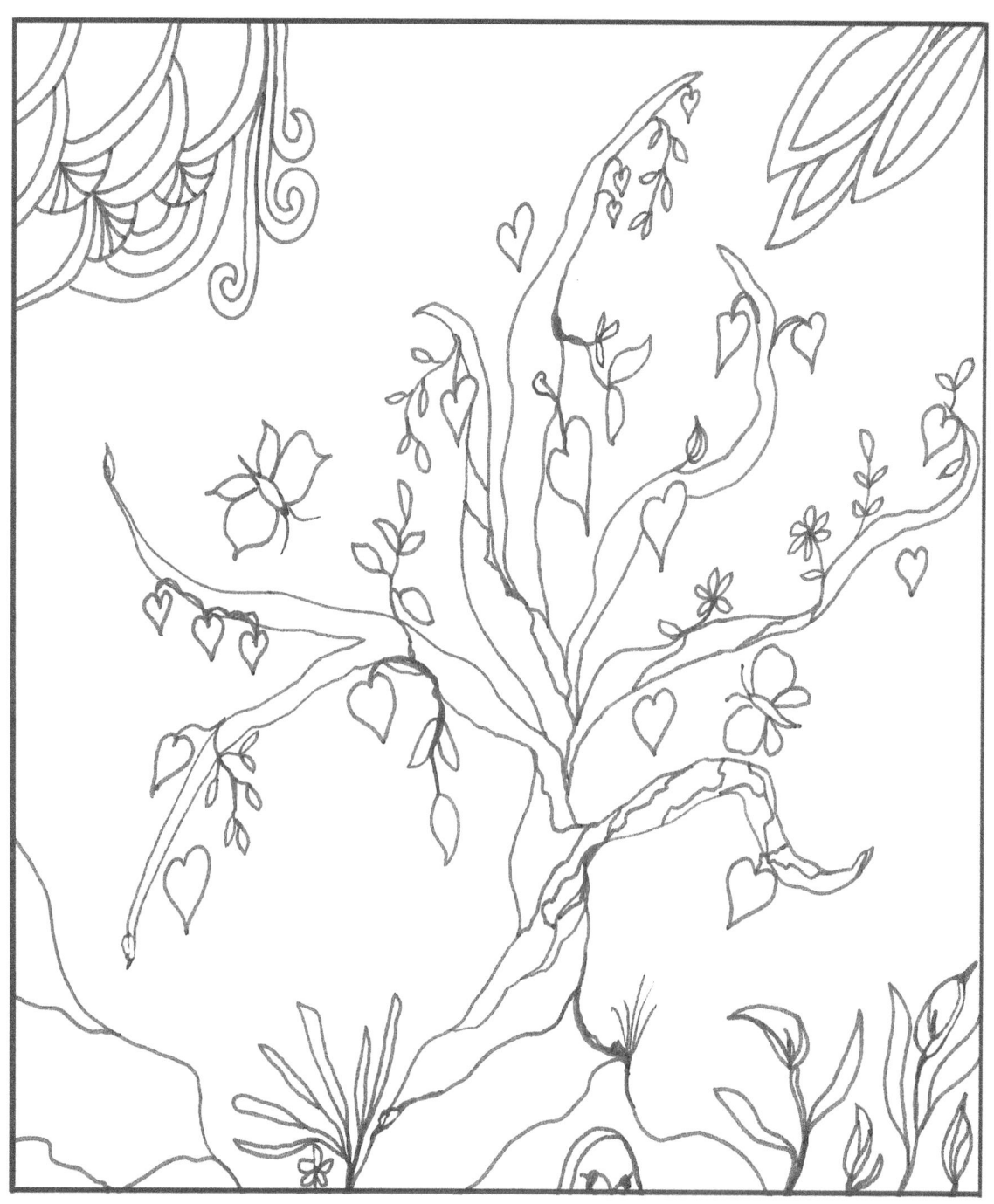

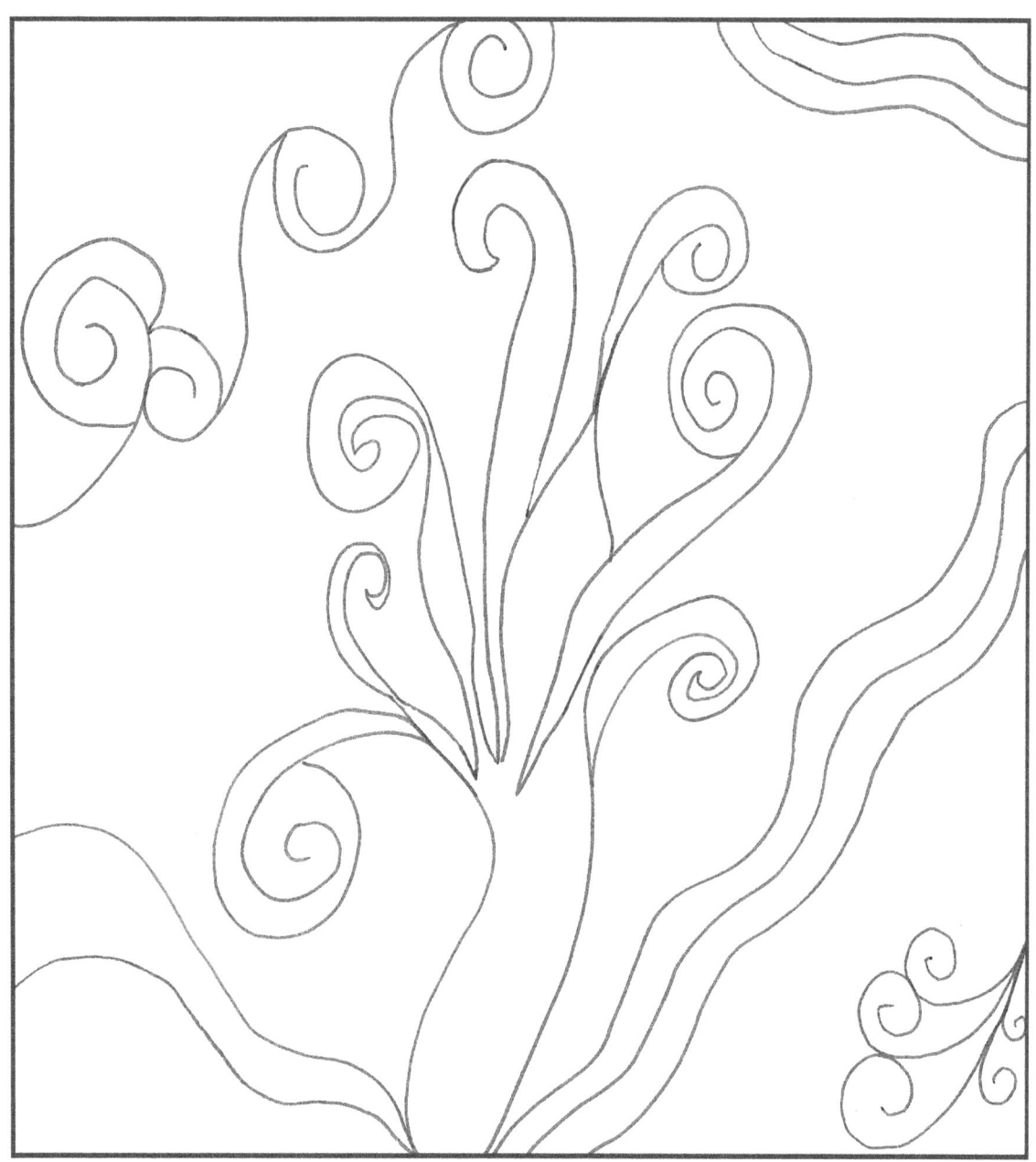

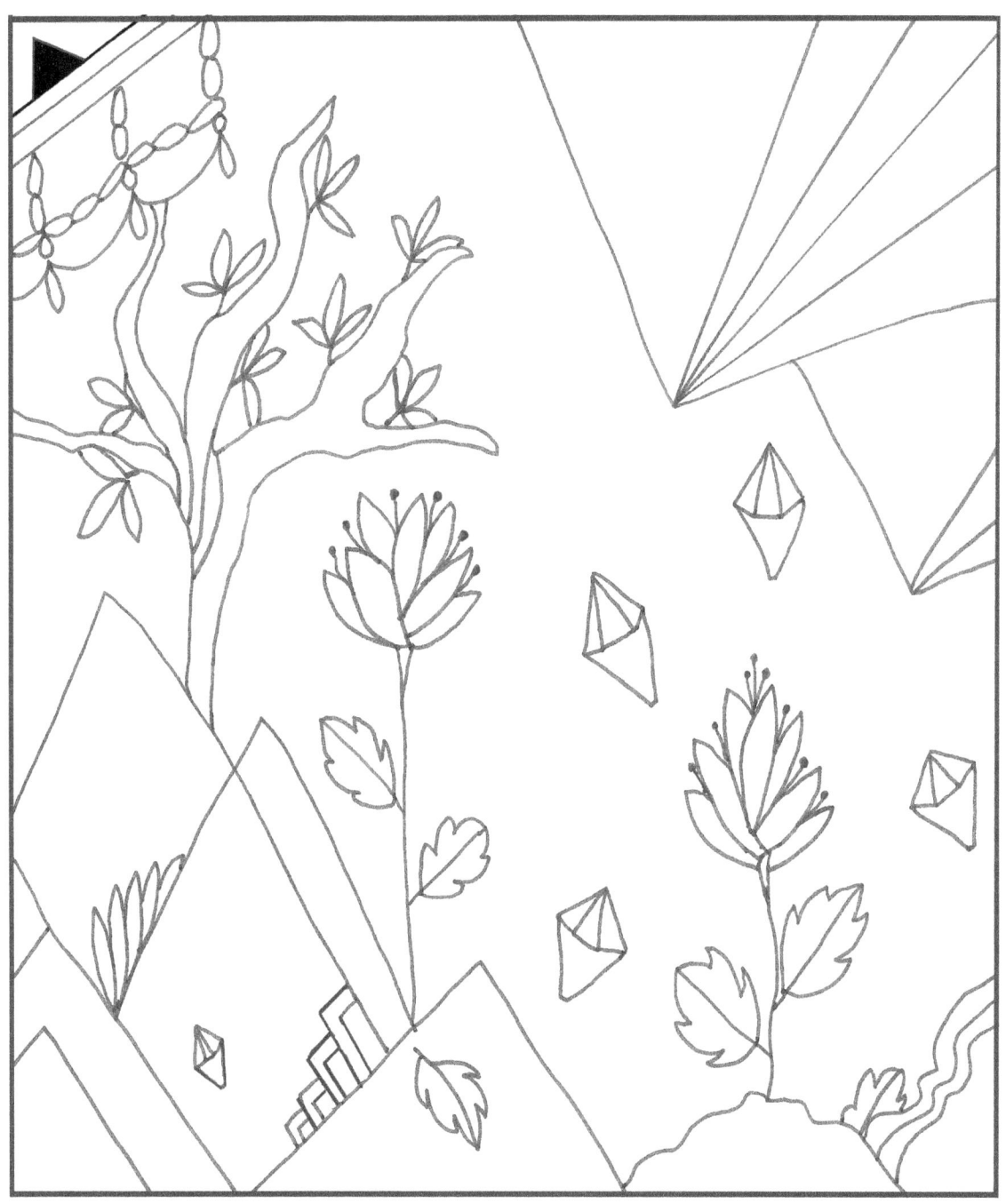

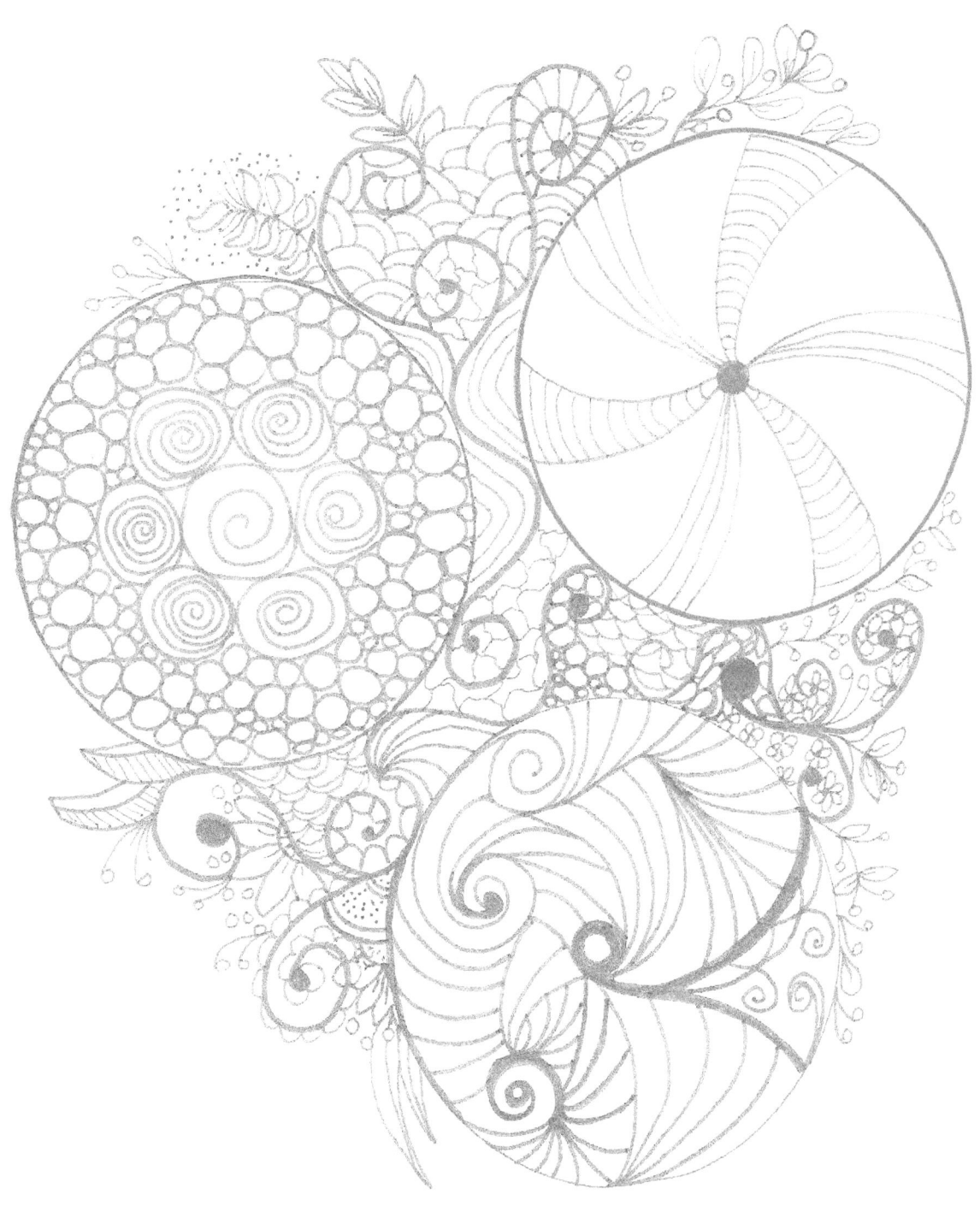

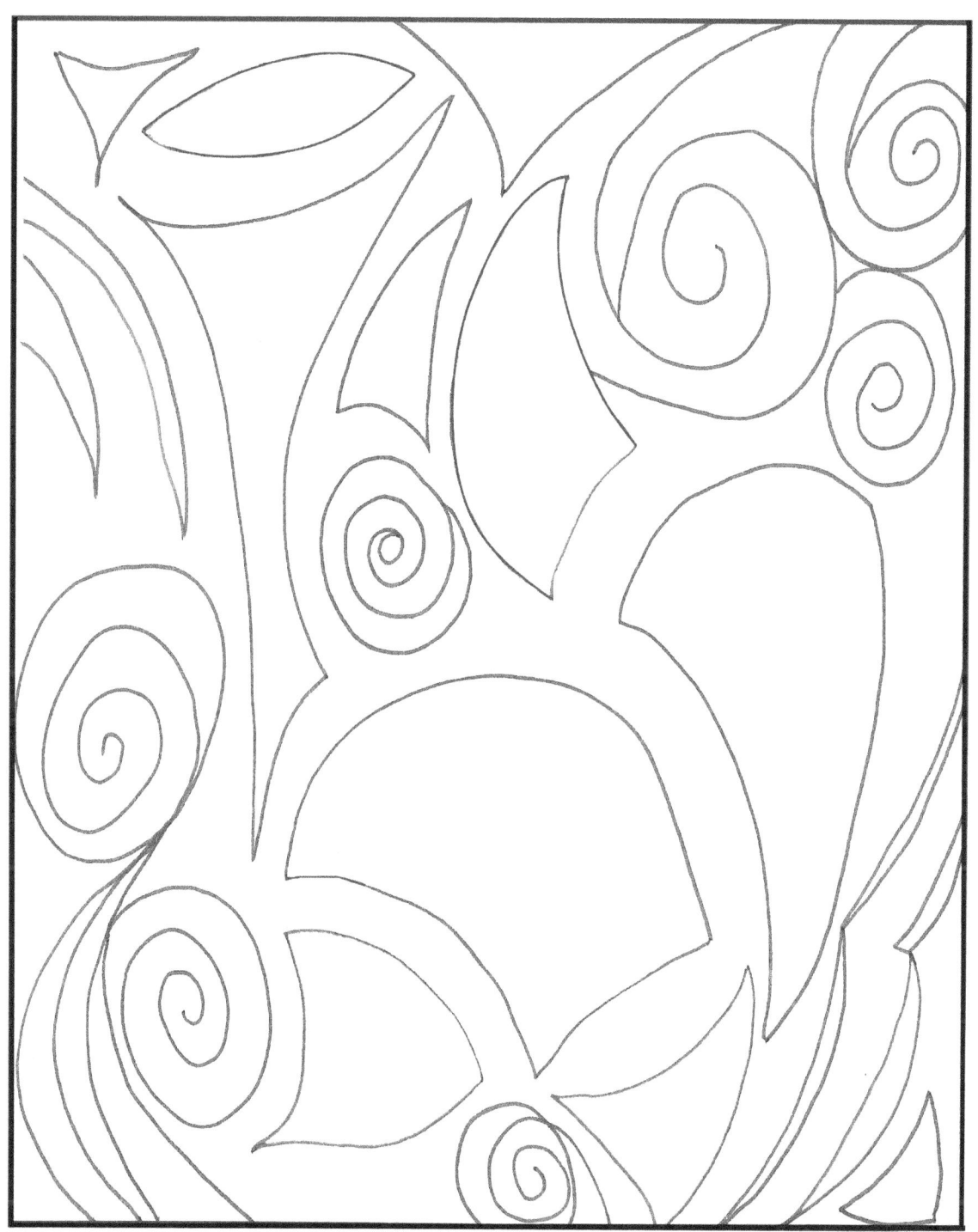

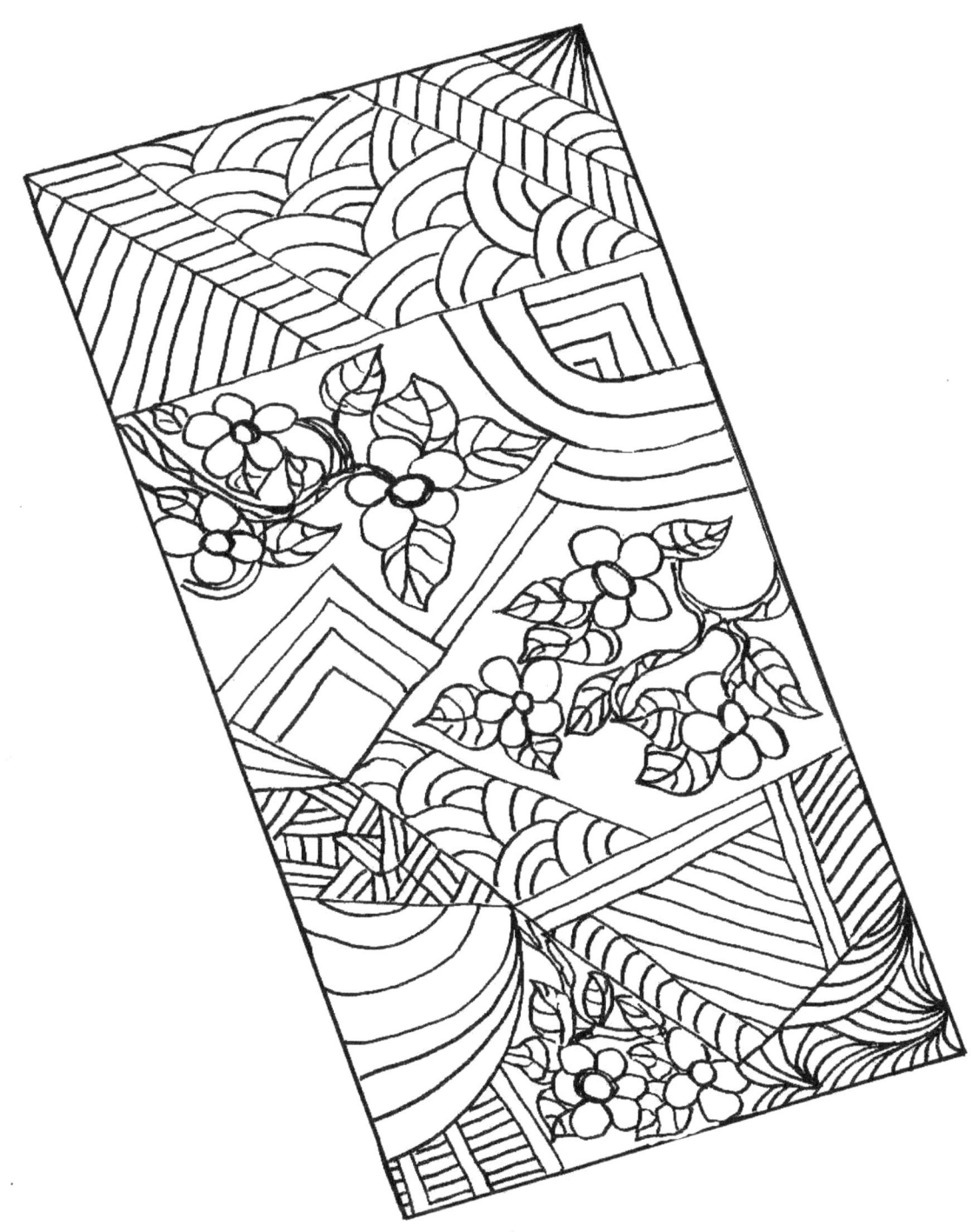

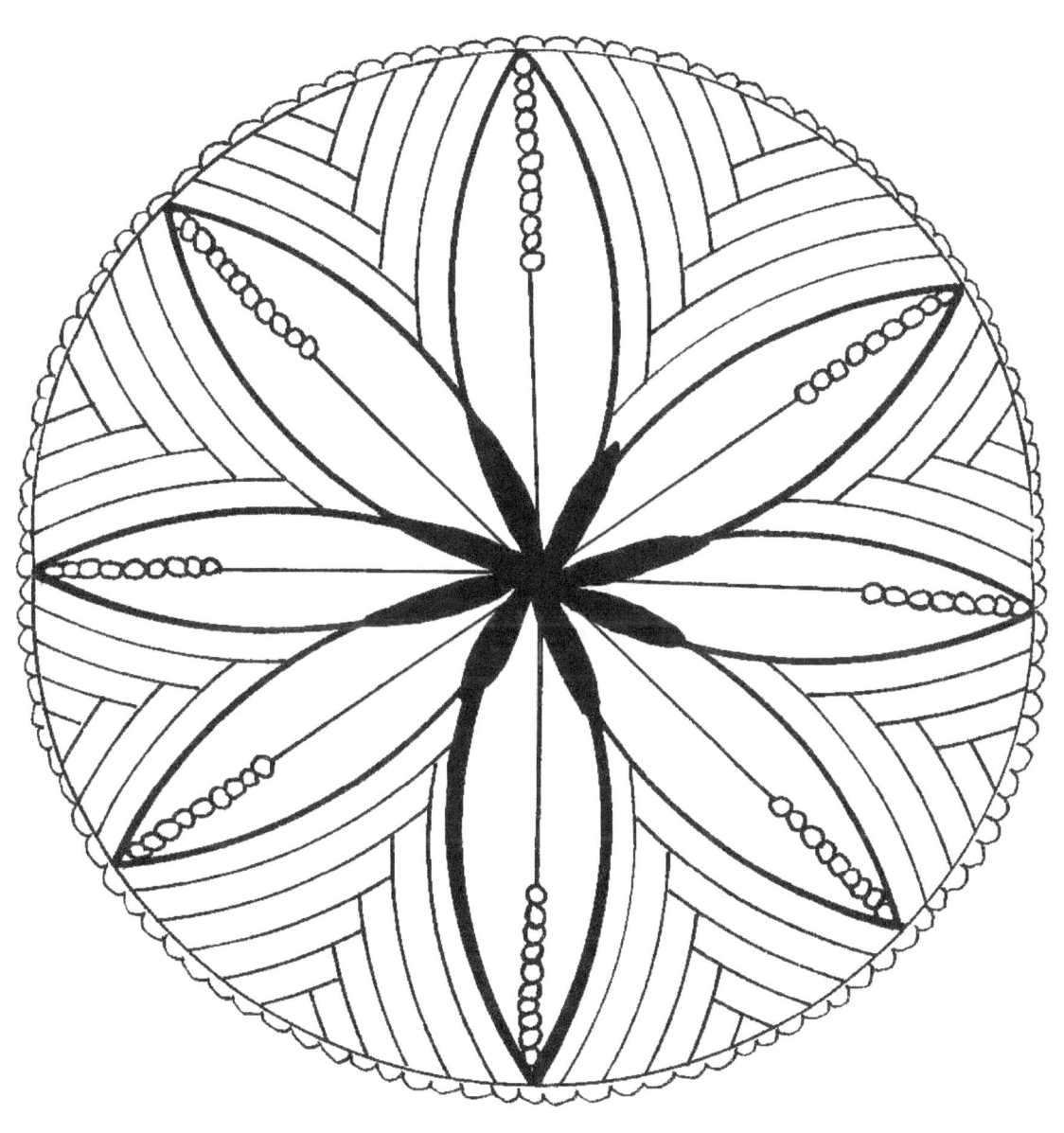

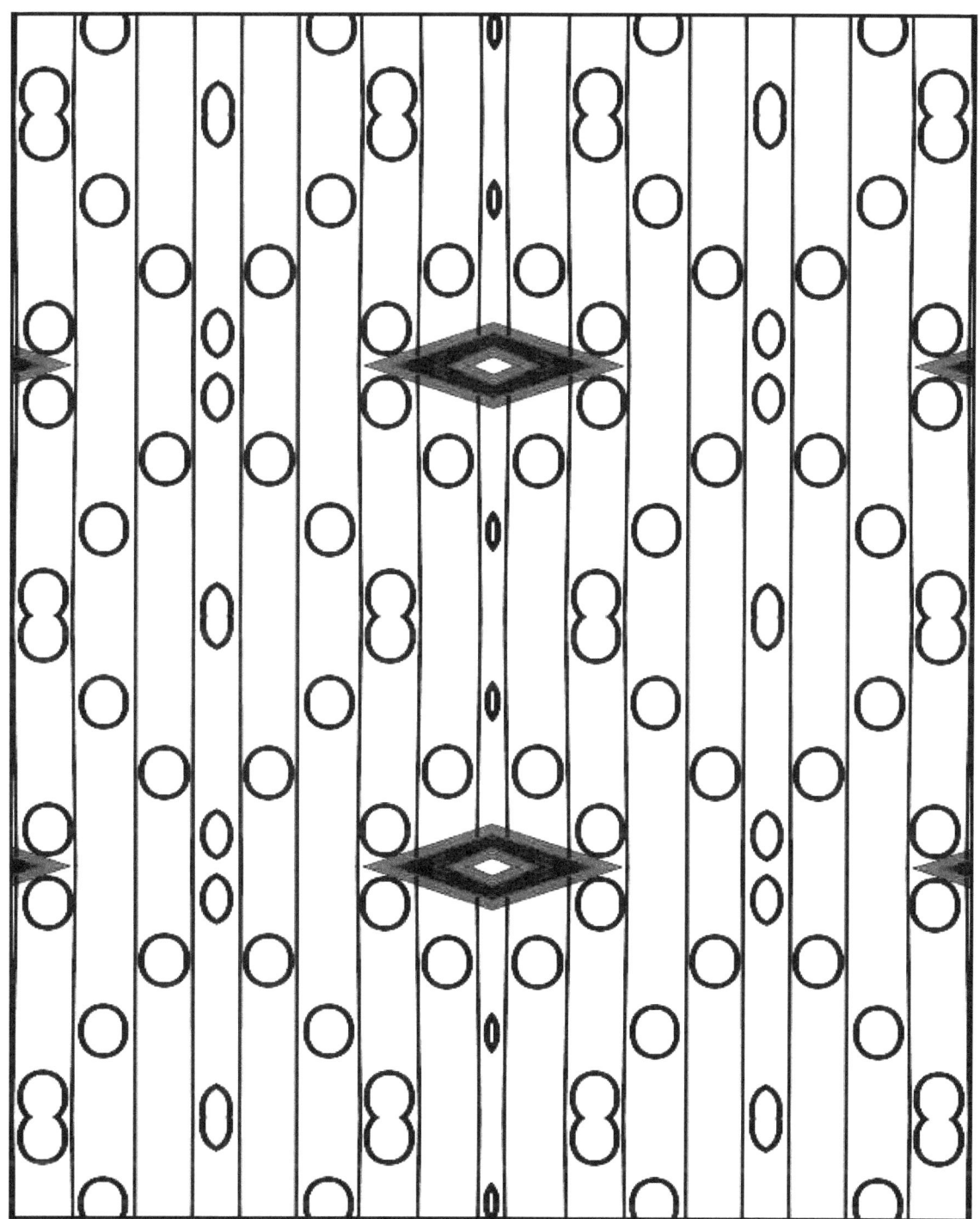

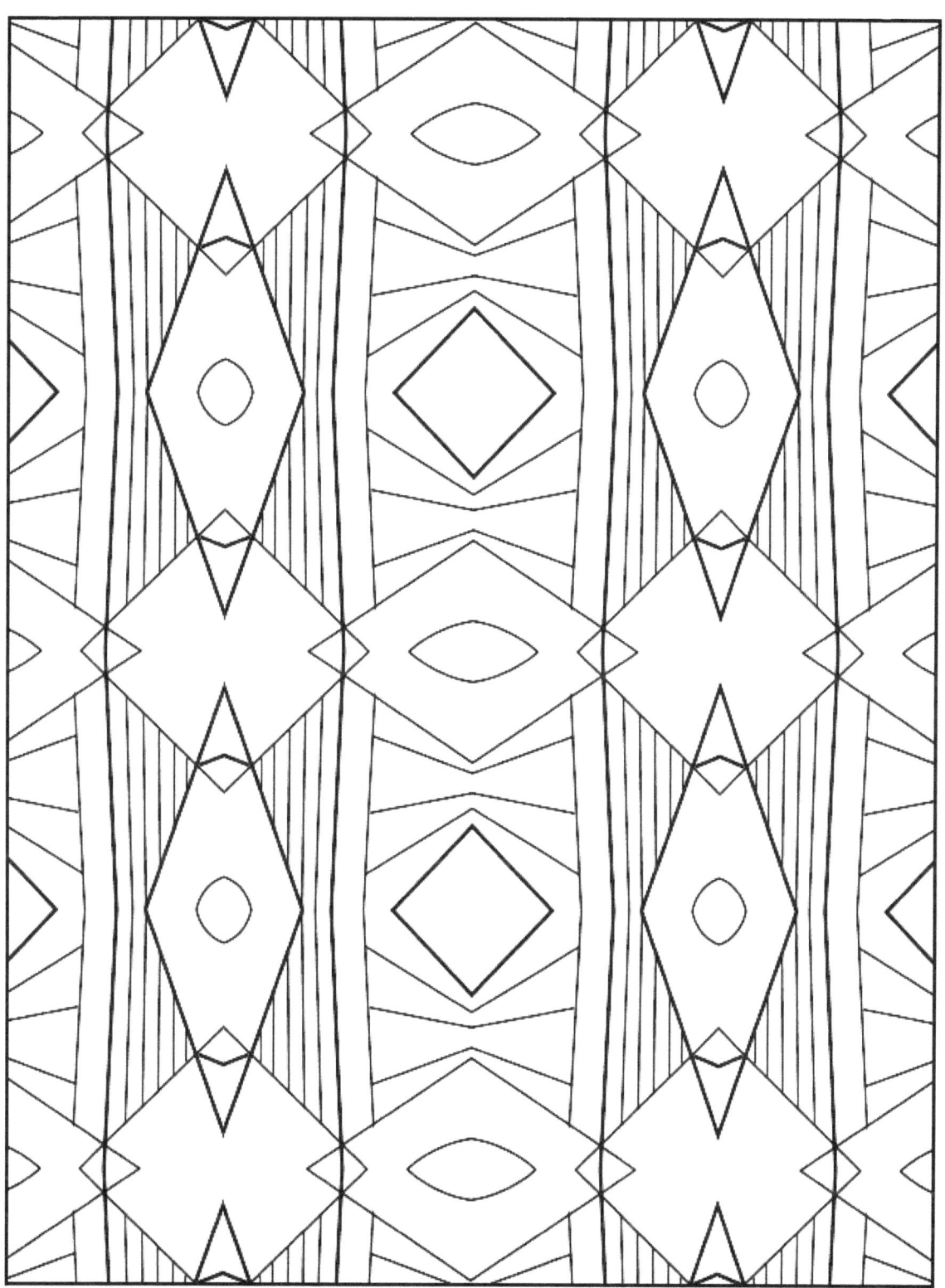

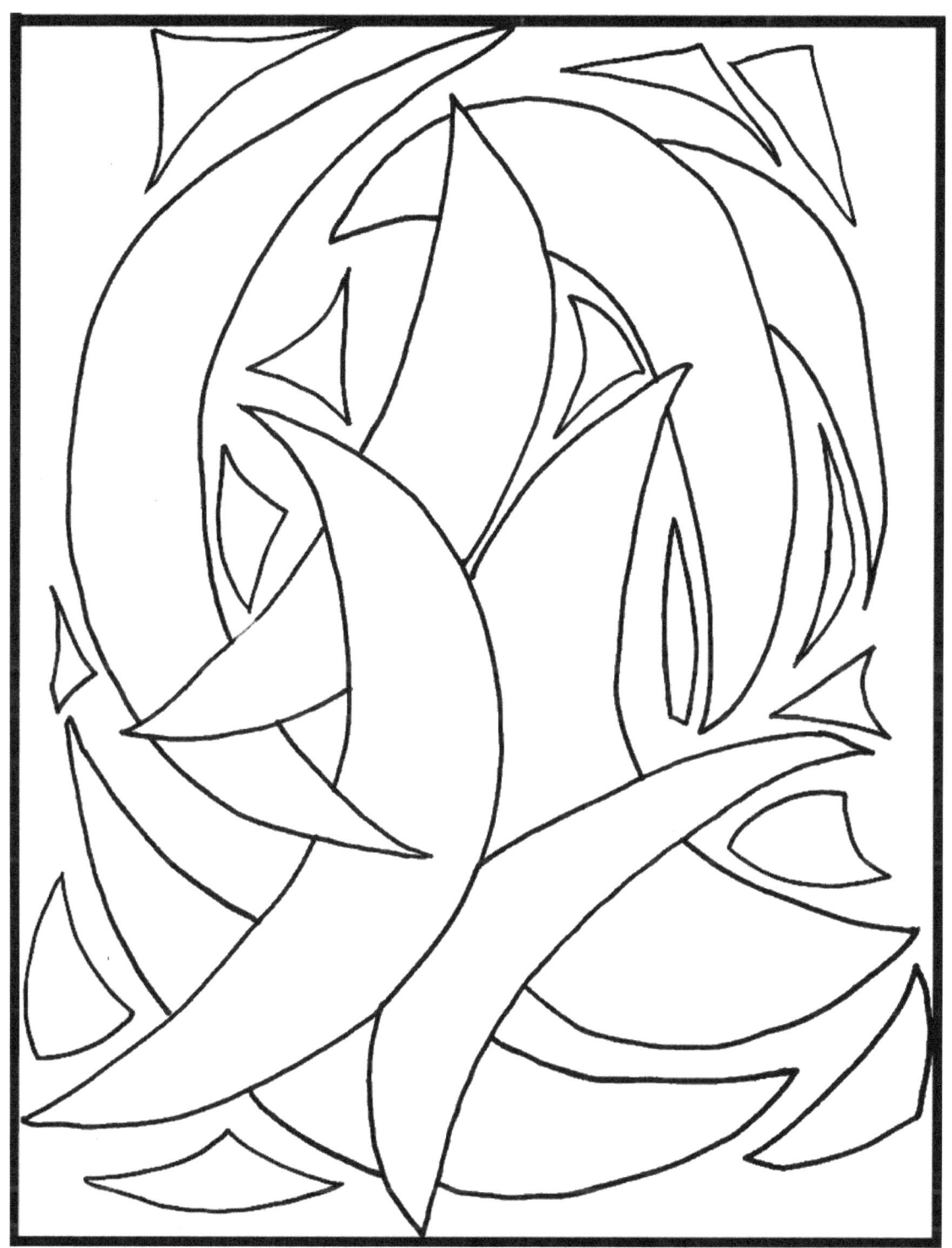

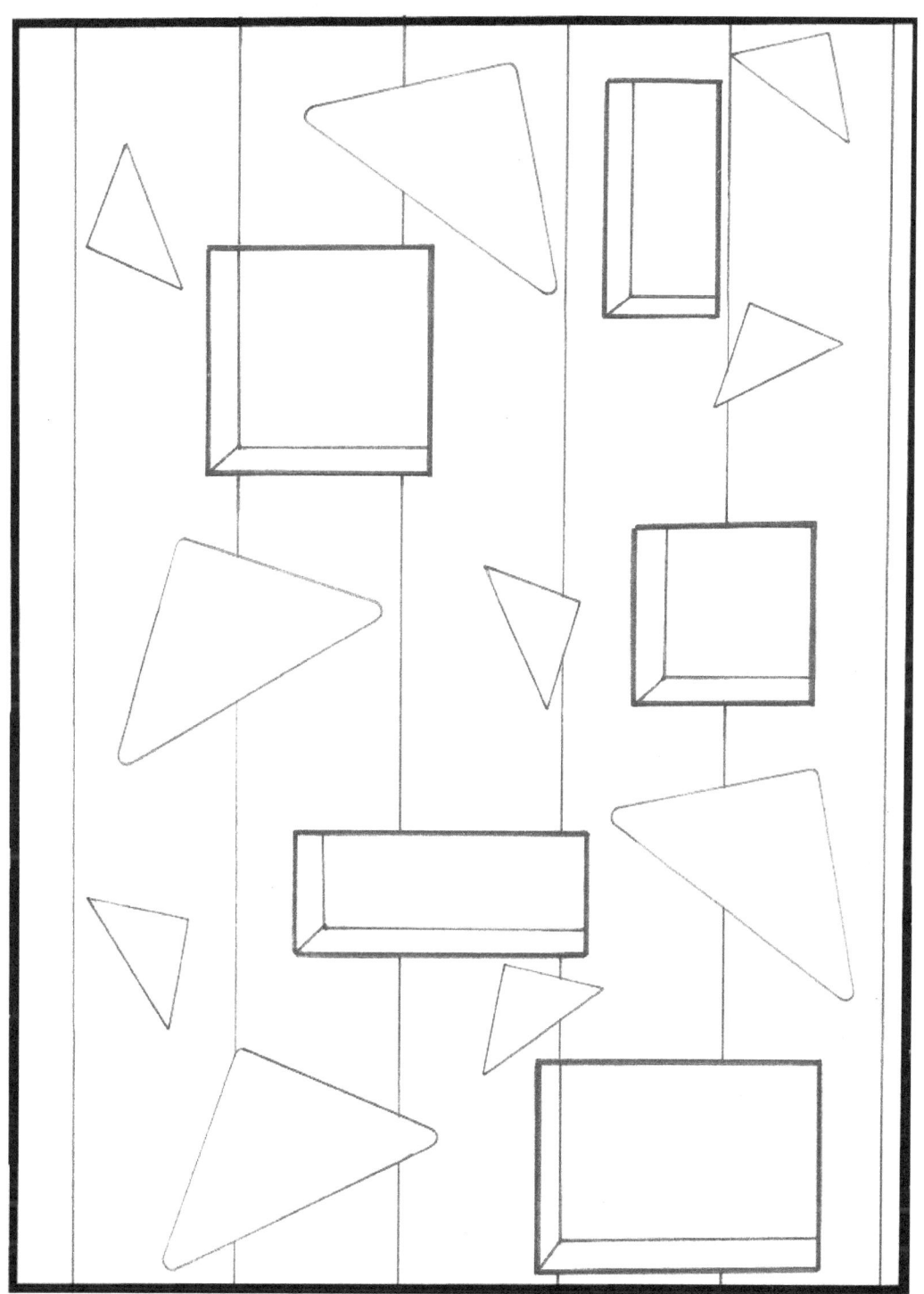

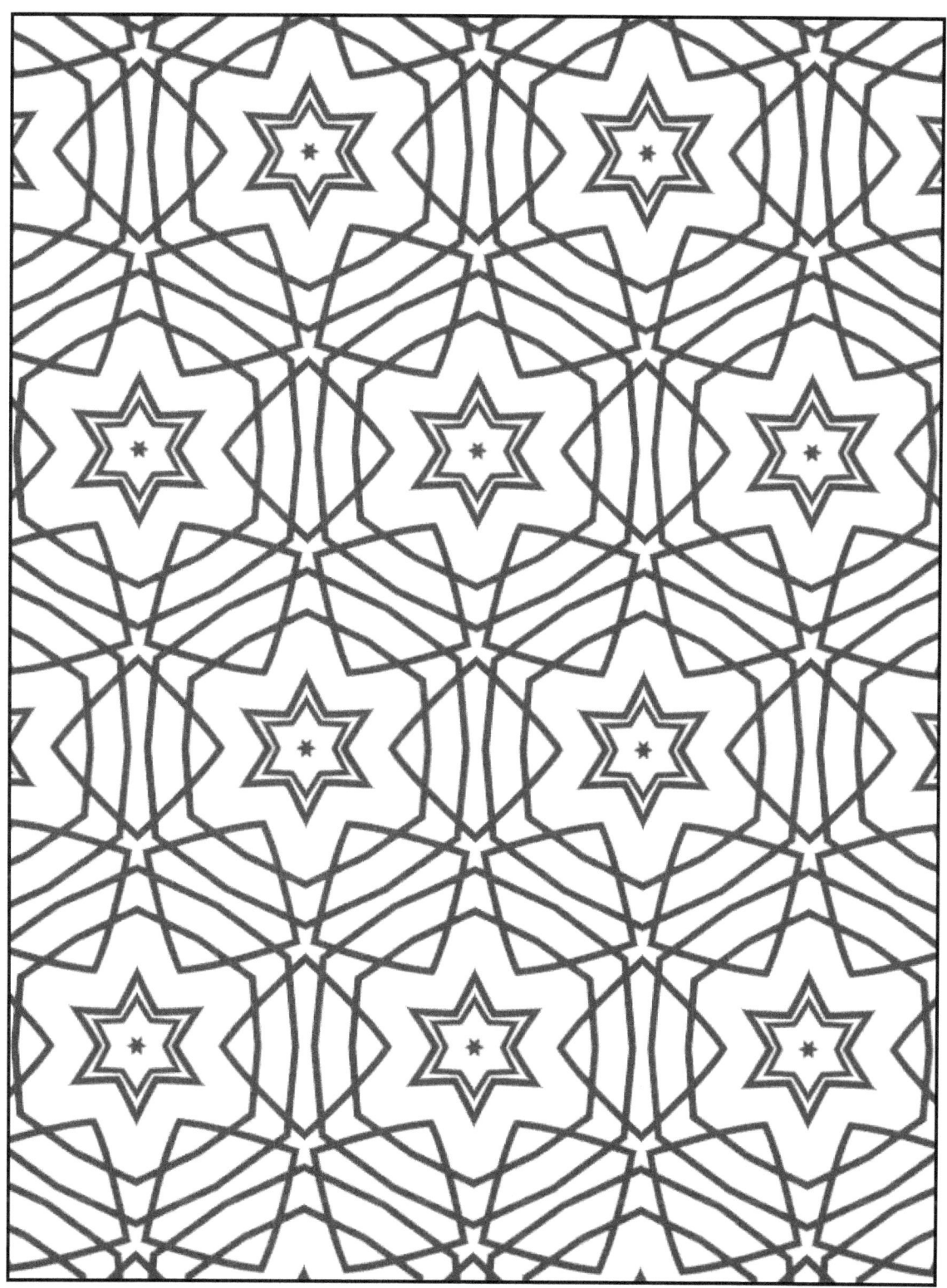

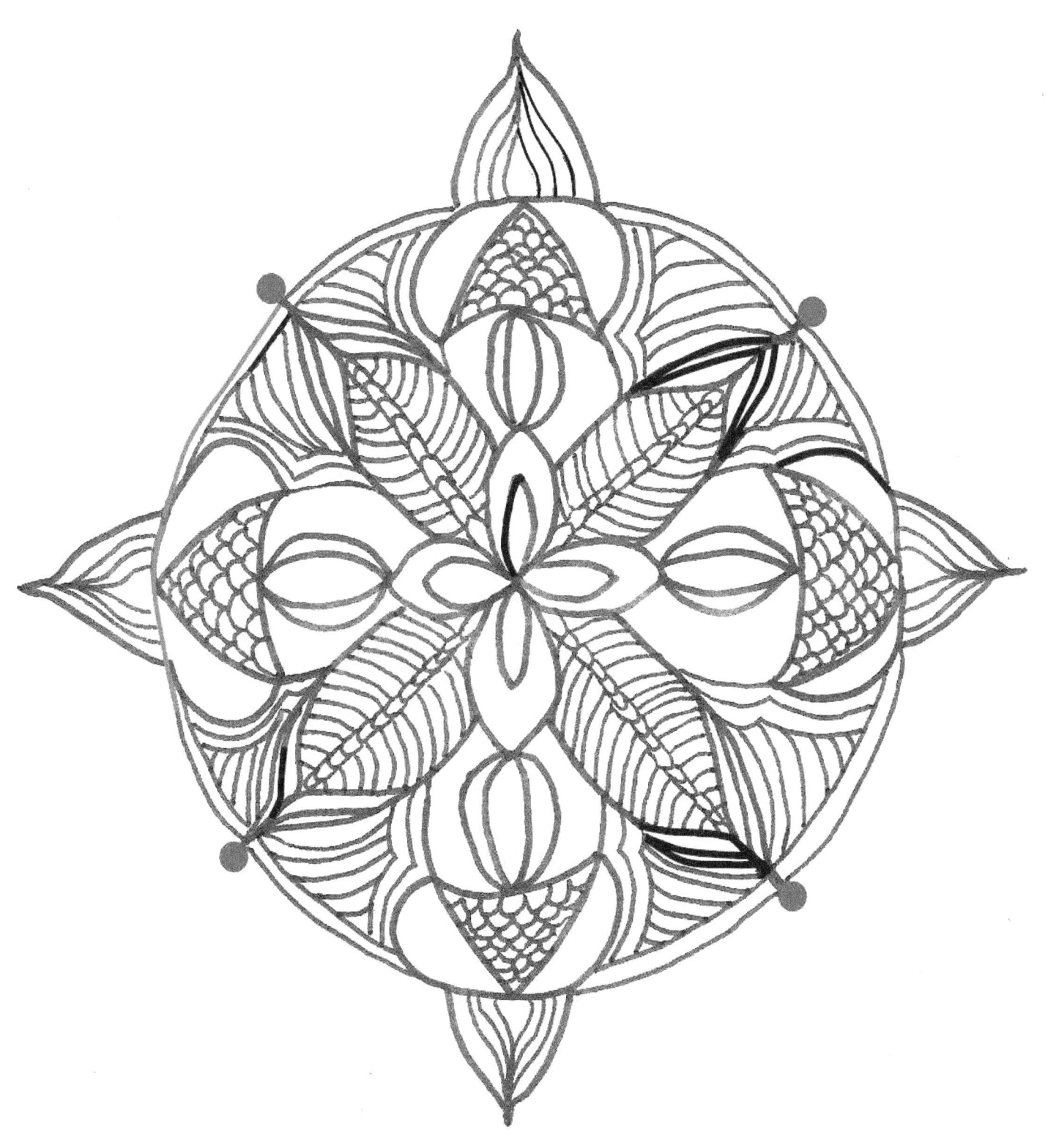

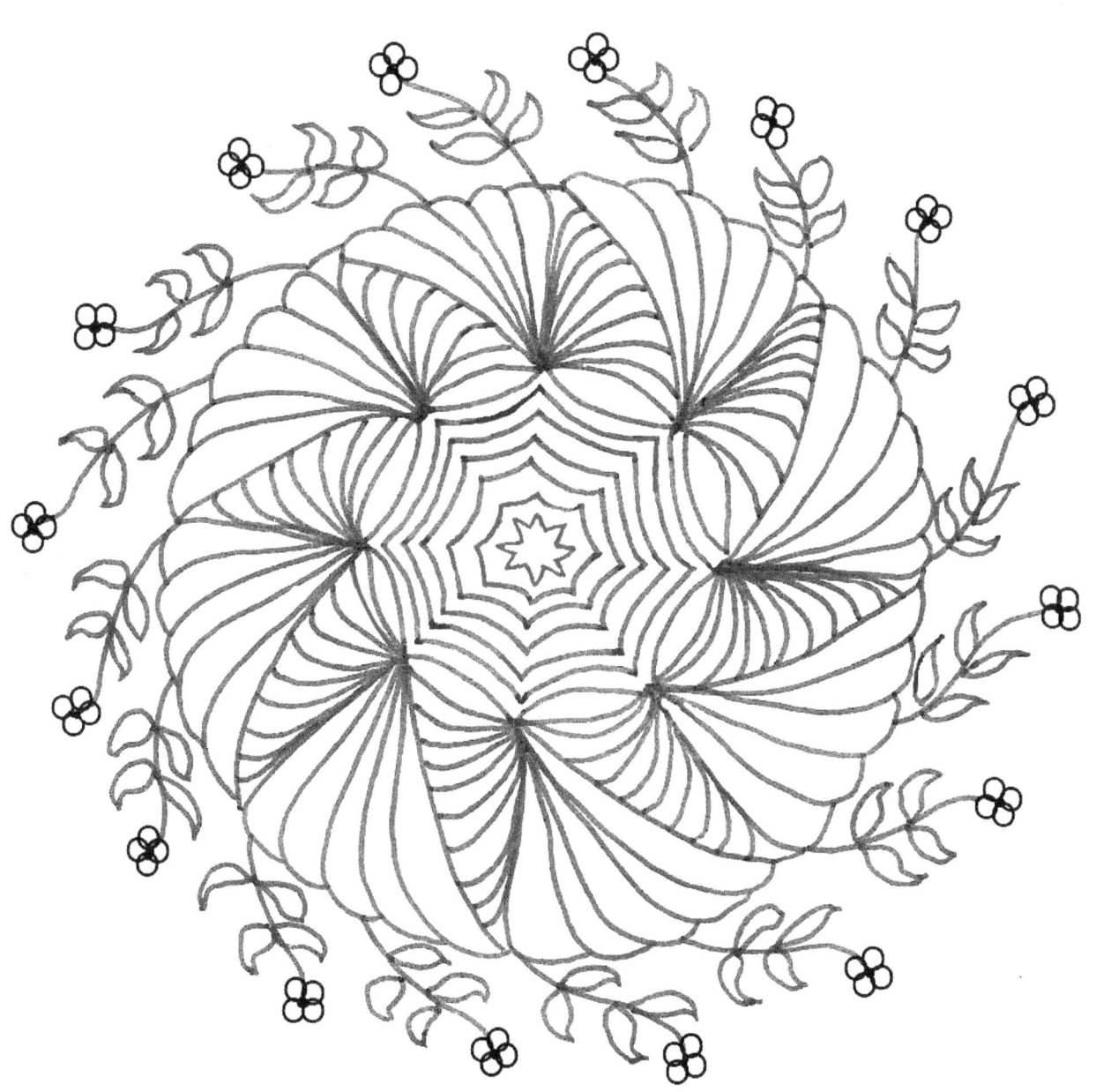

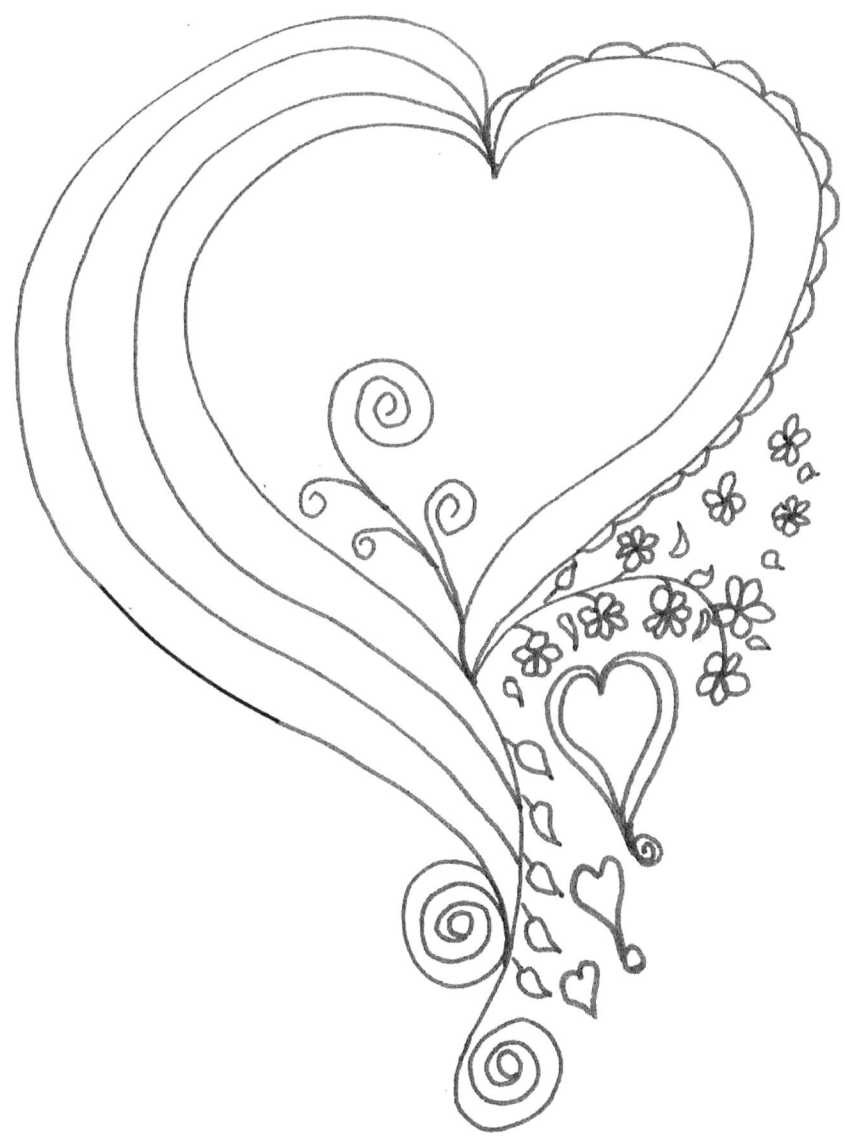

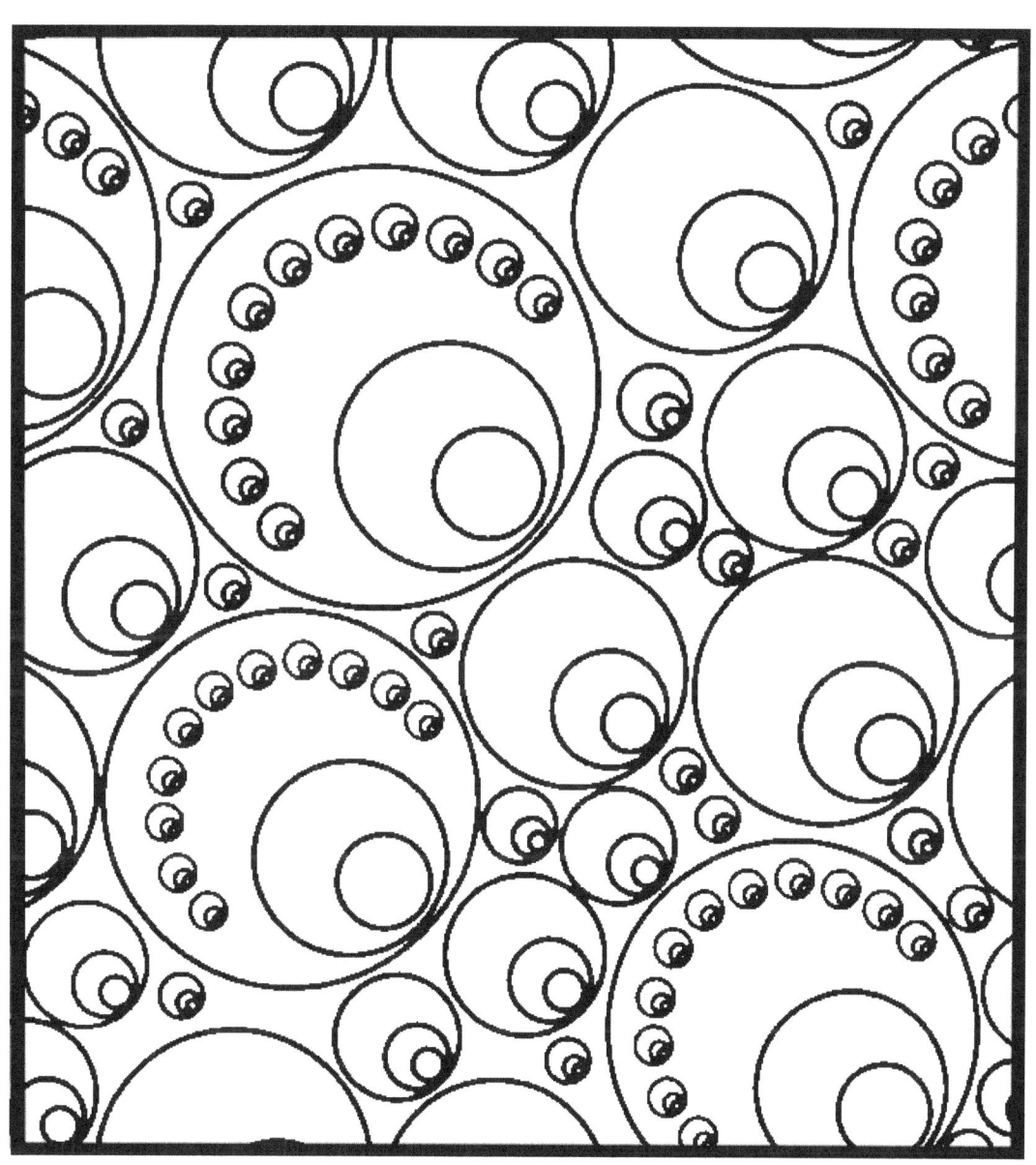

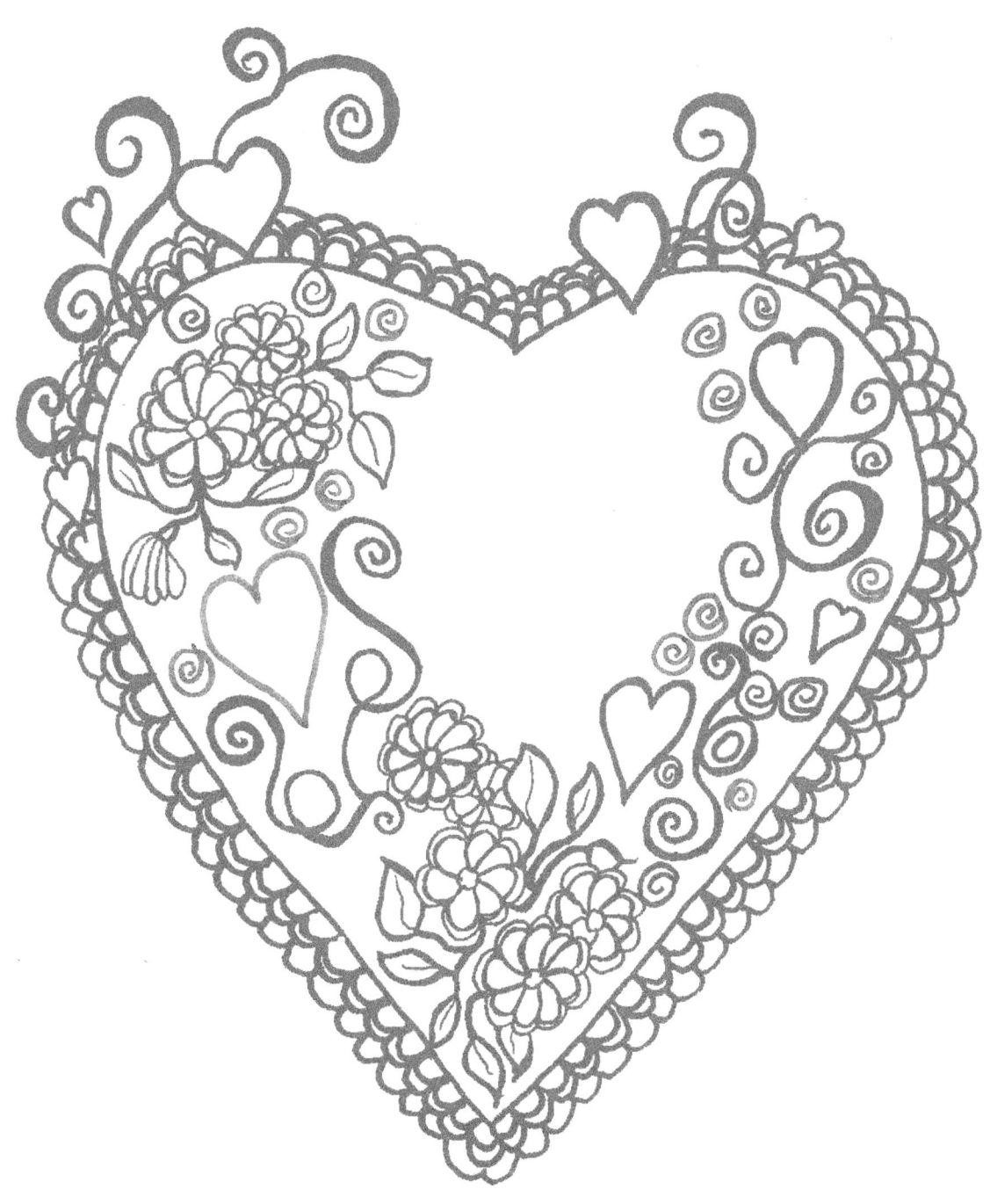

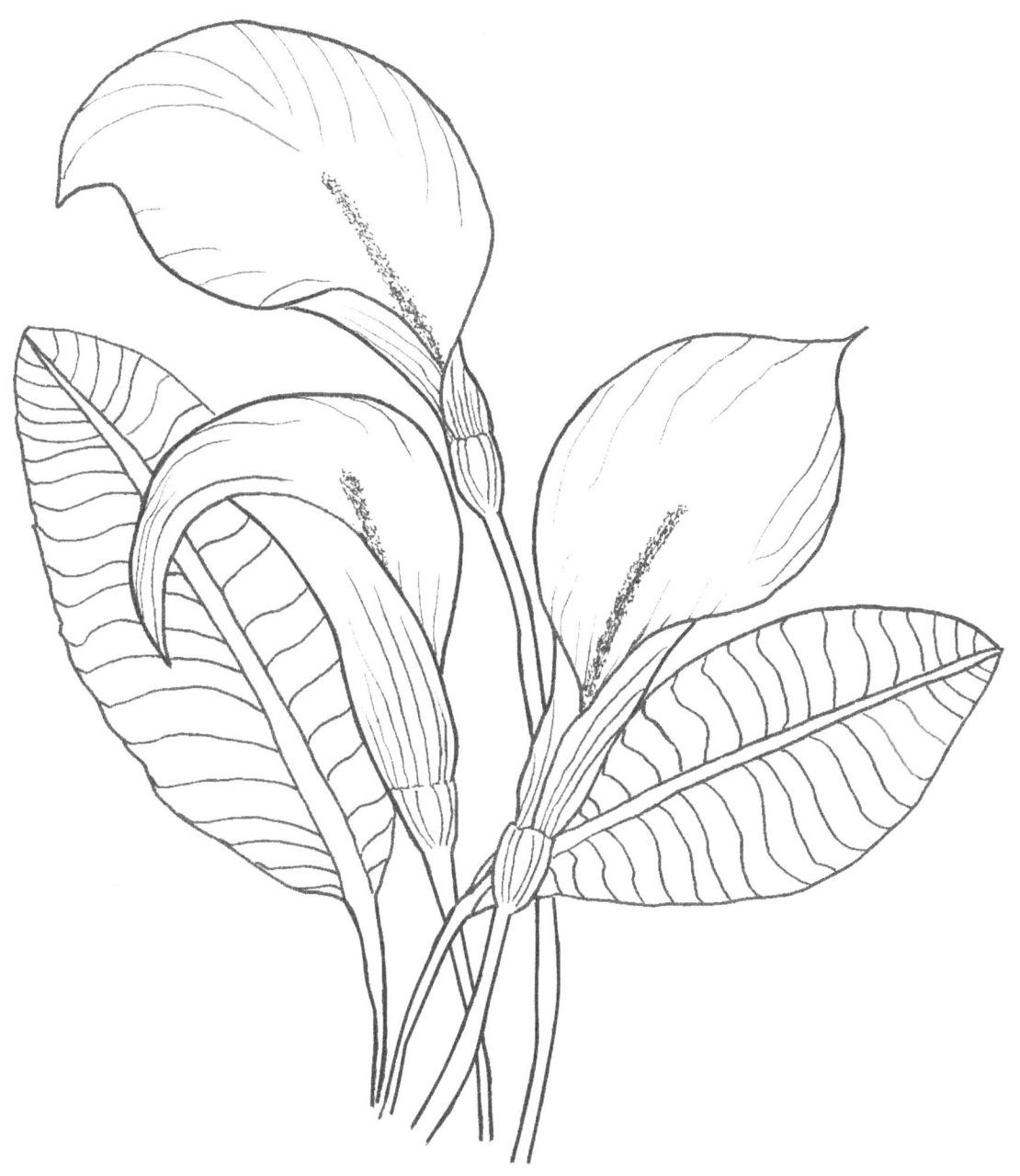

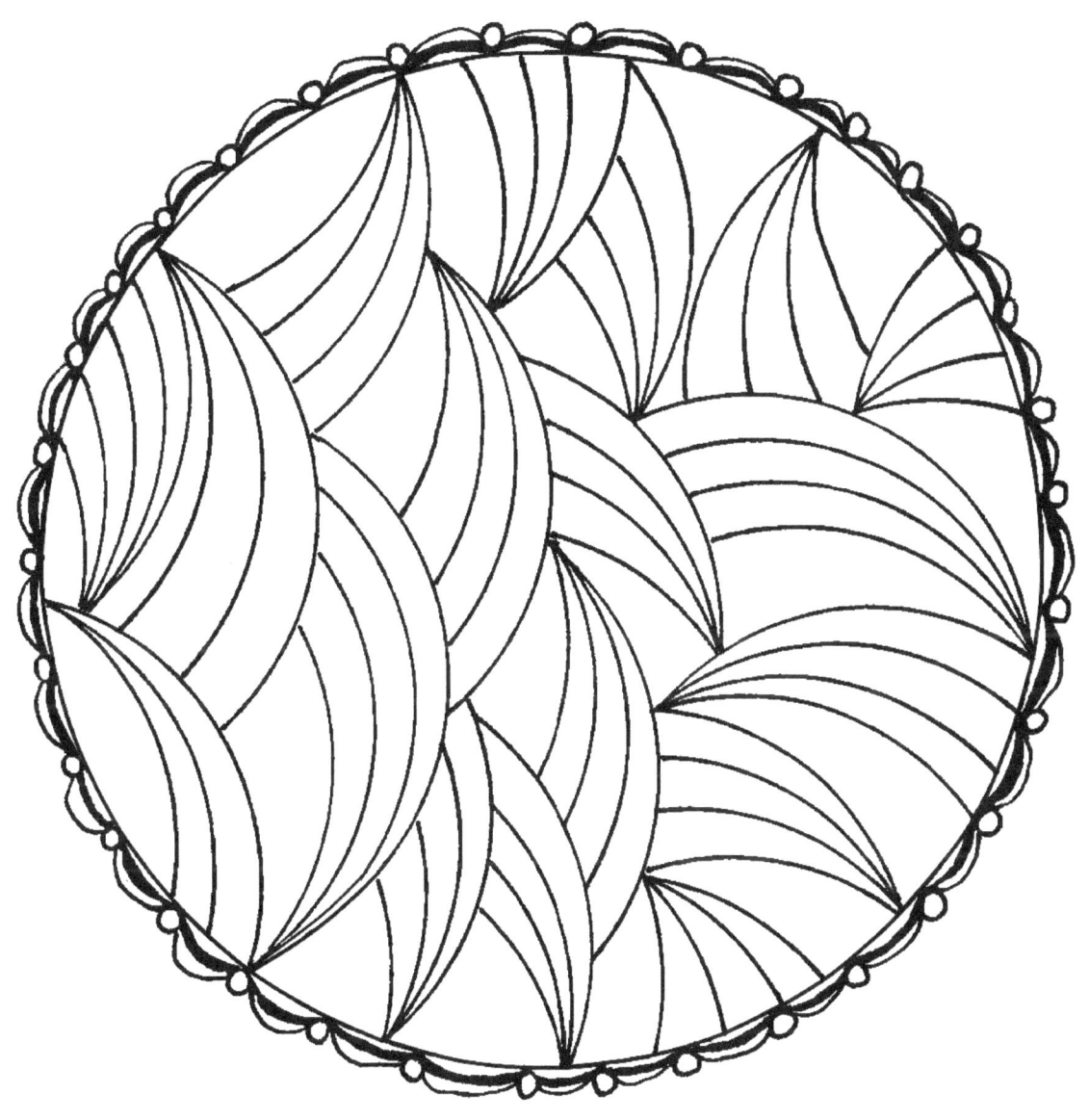

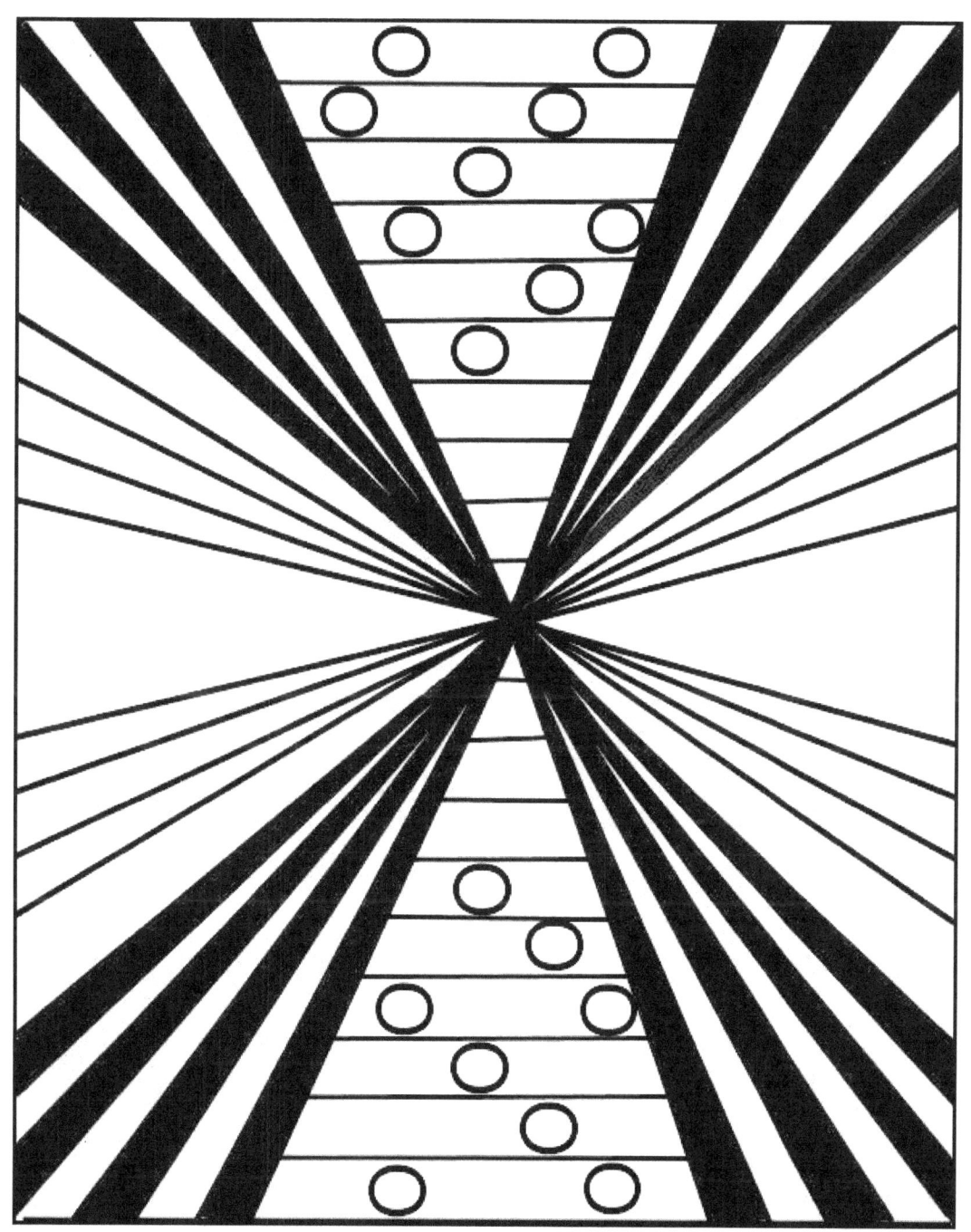

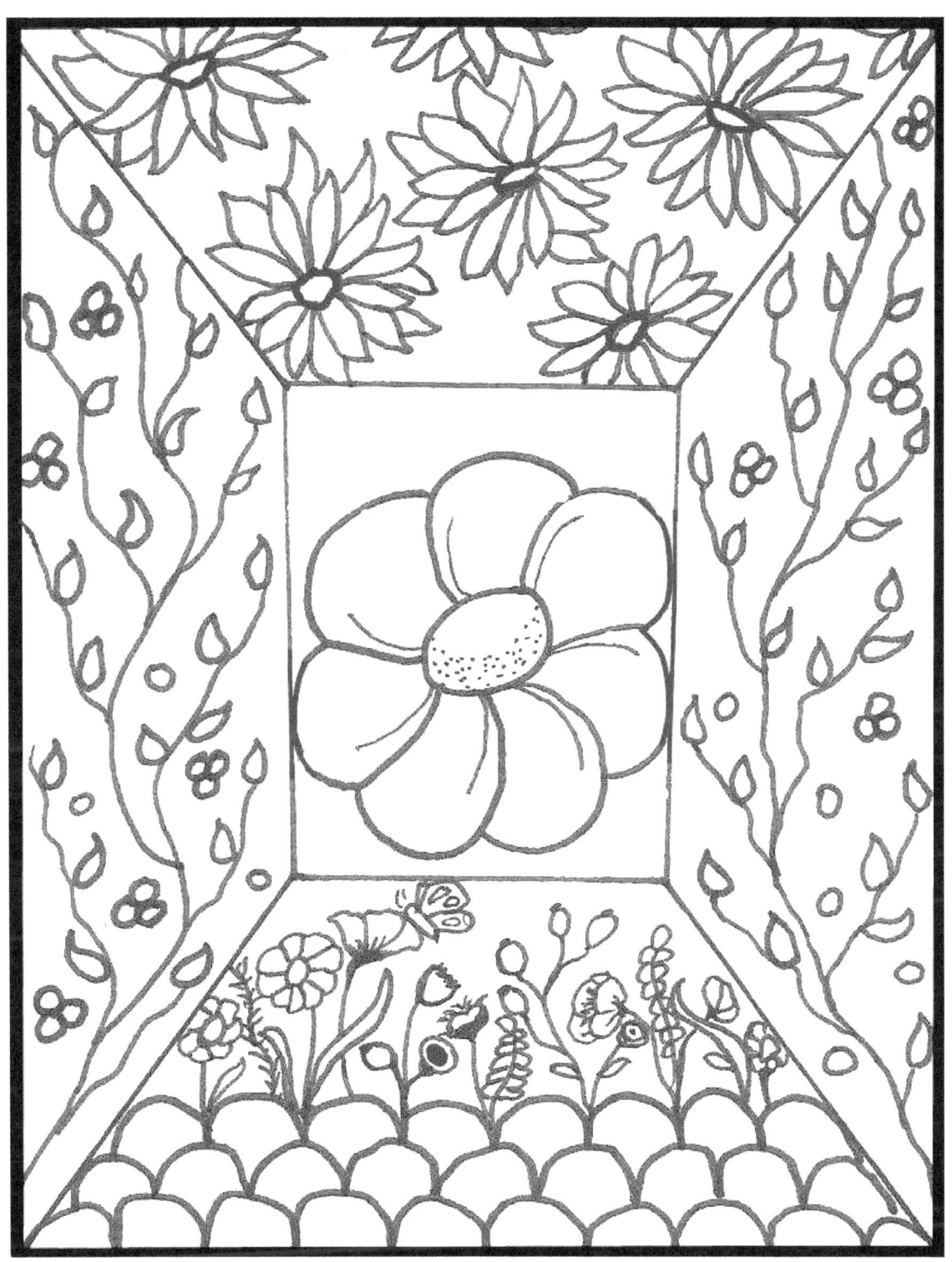

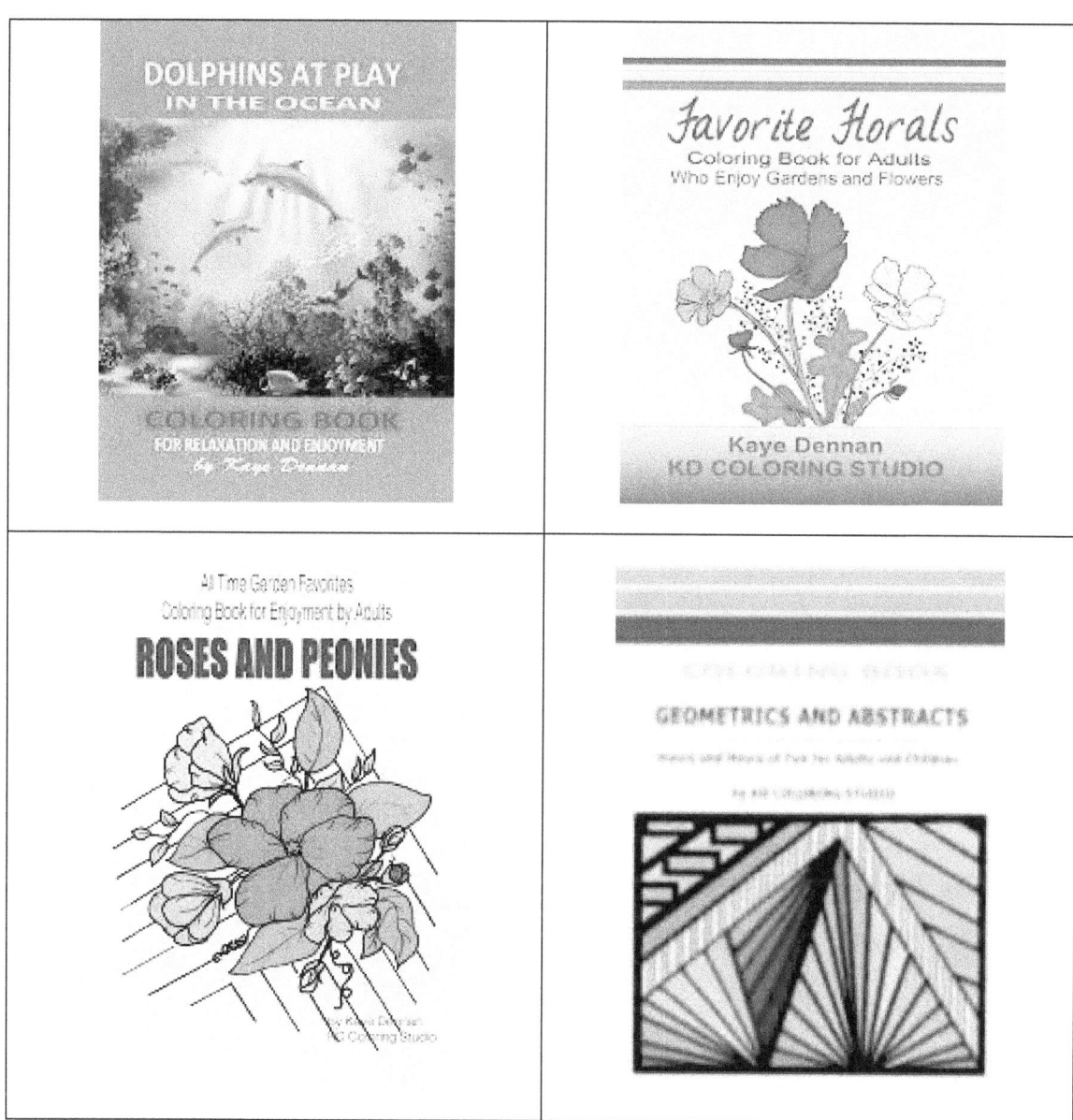

More paperback coloring books can be sourced through

**KD COLORING STUDIO** AT

http://kdcoloring.com

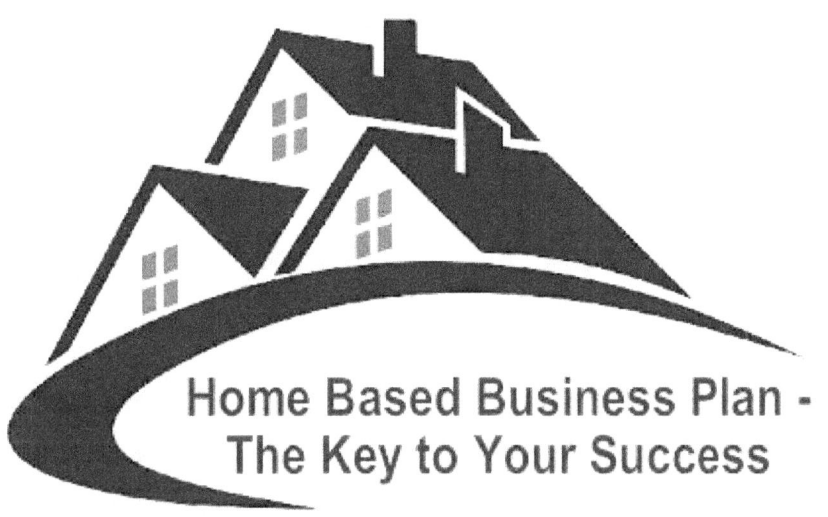

Home Based Business Plan -
The Key to Your Success

## Home Based Business Courses

### by Kaye Dennan
### Author and Home Business Expert
### http://thehomebizcafe.com